ACORNS FROM OAK TREES

Lifetimes of Karma

JYOTIKA ELLWOOD

BALBOA.PRESS
A DIVISION OF HAY HOUSE

Balboa Press books may be ordered through booksellers or by contacting:

Balboa Press
A Division of Hay House
1663 Liberty Drive
Bloomington, IN 47403
www.balboapress.com.au
AU TFN: 1 800 844 925 (Toll Free inside Australia)
AU Local: (02) 8310 7086 (+61 2 8310 7086 from outside Australia)

Print information available on the last page.

ISBN: 978-1-9822-9063-4 (sc)
ISBN: 978-1-9822-9064-1 (e)

Balboa Press rev. date: 03/29/2025

I have written this book for all those people
who are in search of the Truth.

CONTENTS

"I listened to my ancestral voices from the Dreamtime."

KEN'S STORY

In August of 1985 I was working with an exploration drilling company, Weber Drilling, searching for oil in the Great Sandy Desert of Western Australia, we were in an area about 100 kilometers northeast of Marble Bar and 25 kilometers from Callawa Station on a road that linked up to the Wapet Track. The Wapet Track runs from 30 kilometers south of Sandfireplains Roadhouse, 300 kilometers north of Port Hedland, out to Lake Dora in the Great Sandy Desert, about 500 kilometers away and is served well by regular water wells along the track but is narrow and rough in places.

After drilling two exploration wells out near Lake Dora, we moved the rig closer toward Callawa Station to drill the third well, this was to be the last in this area before moving to Geraldton for more work there.

The weather at this time of the year is warm but cool at night so altogether quite pleasant, good conditions to work in and the drilling progressed quickly and without incident. I was the drilling supervisor at the time so appreciated the fact everything was running smoothly as it gave me time to look around the surrounding area. It was an area of flat-topped mesas with extensive flat plains and occasional gullies washed out by the rain with beautiful colours of reds through to white in places. I had been told that Callawa Station was given to and managed by the Martu People, as this area was rich in their history and very symbolic to them and, in fact we had occasional visits from people travelling through to Marble Bar and then back to the Lake Dora area.

Talking to a local from Marble Bar he told me there were a lot of caves with indigenous rock art around the place, so I decided next time I had an opportunity I would go out and have a look to see if I could find some. A few days later we were waiting on a cement job to set so I took my chance and drove down the road to a group of hills I had seen off the road about ten kilometers away, it was early afternoon and with the suns shadow I could make out a couple of caves in the distance, more like large overhangs than caves, but they looked promising, so I turned off the road and drove about a kilometer towards them. I then walked the rest of the way, grateful for my work boots, as the spinifex was quite dense and as most know very sharp spines on the bushes. As I got closer, I realized the cave was quite large. It was up a small rise to the overhang area but easy to climb.

When I entered the area of the cave it was about 15 meters long and varied in depth to 7 or 8 meters, the back walls were covered in paintings of people, kangaroos, emus, and all sorts of other animals, still very sharp in detail with no fading apparent, it was as if they had just been done. I guess its north facing aspect had sheltered them from the elements. Looking around I noticed a grinding stone among the other rocks; as well as a place where the fire was surrounded by stones, as the area is well populated by kangaroos and other animals for food. I guess this shelter had been in use by the Aboriginal tribes for a long time.

I left this main cave and checked out a couple more not too far away but found no further evidence of them being used so I returned to the first cave and decided to take the grinding stone with me. It was quite heavy, so I was happy to get back to the vehicle.

Over the next week I went back to the main cave three times and searched many other promising overhangs in vain, there was always something wrong, not facing the correct way, not deep enough etc. etc. therefore not used by any tribe. We left the area shortly after and I brought the grinding stone back with me to Perth. I have not had the opportunity to return to the cave since but can still picture the place quite clearly.

Acorns from Oak Trees, Lifetimes of Karma

Ken showed me the Aboriginal grinding stone, and then he placed it in the backyard of our house near the swimming pool, amongst some other stones.

Three years later we sold that house in Darlington and built a home in High Wycombe, Western Australia and with all the excitement of the new house, we moved and forgot the stone.

Fifteen years passed and then one day Ken said to me "I wish we had brought the stone with us from Darlington." I said, "What stone?" He said, 'The Aboriginal grinding stone.'

I suggested we go back to the house in Darlington and ask the owners if we could have it, if it was still there. Ken said, "Oh we can't do that."

I decided to go on my own and have a go at getting the stone back to our present house.

I rang the doorbell, and a man opened the door, I told him who I was and that my husband Ken and I had built that house and when we moved, we forgot to take a stone that Ken had found in Marble Bar, and could I please take it now.

He said, "I saw the stone when we first came here and I knew it was different and I wondered why it had been left behind, yes you are welcome to take it."

I took the stone to our house in High Wycombe and Ken placed it under the Jarrah tree.

About two weeks after we had the stone back a friend of mine, Jane, who was sitting near the Jarrah tree waiting for the meditation class to begin came to me and asked me for the name of the CD I was playing, she said it sounded like Aboriginal didgeridoo music. I told her I was not playing any music at the time, nor did I have any Aboriginal instrumental music. She was a bit amazed because she said she could hear it quite clearly.

A few days later two other women told me they heard music in the same spot that sounded like the music Jane had heard.

The following Monday after the meditation class a young man named Marco said he saw an Aboriginal man looking in at the window and asked me if I had any Aboriginal people coming to my meditation classes, I said "No."

Then he said that the Aboriginal man he had seen had white marks on his forehead!

I started to get a bit concerned, my meditation classes were for relaxing and healing the mind, I did not want them to become sessions of strange experiences.

Then a week later another woman "saw" Aboriginal dancers come up to her and it gave her such a fright she had to go outside.

I now began to associate the grinding stone with all these unusual occurrences, because before its arrival in the backyard of our High Wycombe property nothing like this had happened! I had read and heard that Aboriginal people did not like any sacred objects to be removed from their location. Maybe all those years ago Ken had done the wrong thing by bringing the grinding stone to our place in Darlington, some 1476kms south of Marble Bar, its original location.

I decided to get some advice from one of the Aboriginal Elders I had worked with some years before whilst putting together a program to promote Aboriginal culture for primary school students. I phoned his number only to be told by his daughter that he was out, but she took my phone number and said he would call me back, which he did, within the hour, and what he told me blew me away.

The Elder, Ken Colbung, (Nundjan Djiridjakin) spiritual leader and senior clan leader of the Bibulmun tribe, told me that when Ken was in Orissa, India; at this point I almost dropped the phone, how did he have this information? Apart from the people who Ken had worked with, not many others would have known that Ken spent a brief time working in Orissa, and I certainly had not given this Elder that information, there was no need too; I had phoned to find out about the stone. But there was a connection between Orissa and the stone.

The Elder told me that while Ken was in Orissa 'Spirit' contacted him and told him where the stone was and that he was to collect it as he was the 'Keeper of the Stone.' The Elder told me that the spirits of the ancestors were not angry but happy the stone had been brought back to where it spiritually belonged.

He also told me "Eons ago you two were together in the same tribe in Orissa then you two came to be part of this land and now you two are together again but in a different culture."

He went on to tell me that the music and sightings had been 'real' because the Spirits from the Dreamtime had come together and performed a corobboree to celebrate the return of the stone to its rightful owner.

He told me, "Don't worry, they won't come back again."

True to his word, to this day no one has ever heard Aboriginal music or seen tribal, spiritual, people in my backyard.

Neither Ken nor I knew what to make of this 'story,' so we told no one at the time but I developed a new interest in the stone and decided it was going to stay with us forever.

In 2012, about 8 years later I attended a workshop in Coolum, Queensland held by Dr. Brian Weiss on Past Life Regression Therapy. I was overwhelmed by everything I learnt, some information was new to me but most of the information on re-incarnation simply validated what I had already learnt from Swami Umeshranand when I lived in an Ashram in Rishikesh, India.

During the 3 days of the course on Past Life Regression Therapy many people shared their remarkable stories of past-life experiences.

Unfortunately for me a past-life experience did not happen, maybe I was trying too hard? But I was happy I had attended the course because my mind had been opened to so many different things about past lives.

Early in the morning that I was to return to Perth, Western Australia, from Coolum in Queensland, I had a vision/dream – I was in another time and place – I was in the Dreamtime everything was so vivid and clear.

'I could feel the warmth of the sun on my skin and the earth under my feet was a rich red colour that I felt very connected too, almost as if my feet and the ground were one. There were no trees, but the scrub was quite dense, and my feeling of belonging to the land was intense.

Our Leader was Muluwarra, he was strong and larger in size than the other men. He spoke only to the men. There were about 60 in our tribe. I knew I had tied the knot with Muluwarra. When it was time to sleep, I found the right spot for us, and he would come and lie beside me at night; I could feel his body against my back.

We were a silent tribe, in my experience there was not a lot of chattering but there was a connection with each other's thoughts. Words seemed limited when compared to the magnitude of our thoughts.

There was a young man in our tribe whom I felt very connected too. He was about to be initiated into manhood, but Muluwarra became angry with him and speared him in the calf of his right leg.'

In my dream state I felt that pain go right through my leg and then up my whole body.

'The young man did not utter a sound. The spear was left protruding out of his calf.

In my mind I knew why he had been speared. He had had intercourse with a young girl who was to tie the knot with a young man Muluwarra had recently initiated. No one talked about the 'spearing,' but we all knew he had violated the laws of our ancestors.

Muluwarra told us we were moving we knew he knew where he was going. Before moving on he removed the spear from the young man's calf. Another woman and I got some sticky white sap from a thorny bush plant and as soon as Muluwarra got the spear out we pressed our hands down onto the hole in the young man's calf. There was no blood.

The walk was long, in my dream state it was effortless, I could feel the rhythm of the earth and I walked to that rhythm. There was no conception of time.

One day whilst walking Muluwarra who had always been at the front of our small procession, walked back to me and communicated to me, "you are slowing down."

I said "yes."

He looked at me, it was a question. I said, "I have a fever."

He said, "I will get you something."

We kept walking on without him.

After a while I felt my whole body burning up (this experience was physically happening to my body whilst I was asleep), it just got hotter and hotter like I was on fire.

Then a glorious coolness and I was floating above my body. I vividly remember feeling so cool and light as I hovered above my dead body. The tribe moved away from my body, but I hovered above it.

Muluwarra returned to my body that was lying down on the red earth curled up in the fetal position. I felt his despair. In his hand he had yellowish-red berries, and I knew they would have taken the fever away.

He gently picked up my body – I remember thinking how thin and small it was. He carried it to a sandy spot and placed it down. He used a long digging stick to dig a shallow grave, then kneeling he placed my body in it and using his hands he covered it over with sand. Then he placed the grinding stone on the top.'

I woke up from this experience uttering sounds that were completely unfamiliar to me. My tongue was rolling in my mouth fast and 'words' were coming out; I recognized Muluwarra and Yatigiri. Was Yatigiri the name of our tribe?

Then to my horror my fingers were stuck together. At first, I thought they were cramped, but after washing my hands in warm water without them coming apart I wondered if they were part of my experience of the sticky sap? As full consciousness and reality came back to me my fingers opened and I had complete control over them. And with that came the full realization of what I had just experienced, a past life with my present husband Ken, and the stone Muluwarra had placed over my dead body hundreds of years ago, was back with us again in this lifetime, placed under the Jarrah tree in our backyard!

THIS LIFETIME

Ken was born in Midland in Western Australia on 1 March 1943. His mother was an Australian and his father was a migrant from England. He was deeply connected to the land and could go anywhere in the outback and never get lost. He just seemed to know his surroundings. He knew the plants of the bush, where the waterholes were and had a vast knowledge of the birds and animals that were native to the different areas. He loved to travel and go walkabout. Even though he was a 'white' Australian the Aboriginals in the bush always called him brother or bro, his connection with them was unique.

The evening Ken met me in a pub in Perth he said it was love at first sight, he told his mother that night that he had met the girl he was going to marry.

I was born in Jhansi, India to Anglo-Indian parents on the 14 Nov. 1945. We immigrated to Australia in 1964 and became Australian citizens. When I met Ken, in 1966 I was not thinking of marriage, but due to my strong links with India I was hoping to go back to India as soon as I could afford the sea-fare back. But that did not happen because soon after I met Ken, we became engaged and married in 1967.

"Beloved one what joy there is in meeting you again this lifetime."

We were soul mates and were married for 53 years before he died from cancer in 2020. I have no doubt that we will have more lifetimes together. Today the stone sits above his ashes protecting him like it did me, all those years ago.

RE-INCARNATION

Pure soul how long will you travel? (Rumi 1207)

"Surely not in vain my substance from the common earth was taken, that he who subtly wrought me into shape should stamp me back to common earth again." Persian Sufi Omar Khayyam.

"Dehino smin yatha dehe
Kaumaram yauvanam jara
Tatha dehantara praptir
Dhiras tata na muhyati." Bhagavad Gita 2:13

'As the embodied soul continually passes in this body from child, to youth, to old age – the soul similarly passes into another body at death. The self-realized soul is not bewildered by such a change.'

In the Bhagavad Gita 2:27, Hindu sacred text, Lord Krishna told the warrior Arjuna, 'To one that is born, death is certain; and to one that dies, birth is certain. Many a birth have I passed through, and so have you. I know them all, but you know them not.'

Today most of the world's population believe in re-incarnation, the notion that we have lived many lifetimes here on earth. But what is the purpose of it all? It is for the evolution of the soul to the highest level of consciousness, call it enlightenment, the Truth, or Moksha; then instead of the usual pattern of birth, death, and re-birth, our soul will not need to return to earth in another body to learn any more tough lessons, it will find eternal peace in a Heavenly dimension.

The Christian Bible says it thus: 'for they cannot die anymore, those who are counted worthy.'(Luke20:36)

Buddhists say re-incarnation means 'an ever-growing wealth of experience. It means a sometimes difficult and exhausting road to more insight, deeper feelings, richer talents and to being more oneself and more related to others.' Buddhists say that imperfection in this life will lead to less imperfection in the next if we serve with compassion.

For Christians it is to love one another through the sacred heart of Jesus.

From the Hindu sacred text, the Upanishad 3:14

'This Soul of mine within the heart is smaller than a grain of rice, or a barley corn, or a mustard seed, or a grain of millet, or the kernel of a grain of millet; this Soul of mine within the heart is greater than the earth, greater than the atmosphere, greater than the sky, greater than these worlds. Containing all works, containing all desires, containing all odors, containing all tastes, encompassing this whole world, the unspeaking, the unconcerned – this is the Soul of mine within the heart, this is Brahman.'

This now brings us to the significance of karma, everything we experience in our lives today is a result of an action we committed in a past life. Whether we experience abundance or pain and suffering it is the result of karma from a past life.

The Buddha answered it well when a young man asked him, "What is the cause Oh Lord that we find amongst humankind the high born and the low born?" Buddha replied, "It is karma that differentiates beings into high and low states."

To re-invent oneself to a higher level of consciousness, sometimes referred to as the I AM level of consciousness, in each lifetime we need to go deeper into our feelings.

Say these words to tap into a higher level of consciousness:

I AM I AM I AM

I AM Light divine,

I AM Truth sublime,

I AM Love beyond space and time.

I AM I AM I AM

When we connect into our feelings more consciously, we can tap into past life experiences. All our experiences, past and present, are stored as memories in our auric field, or causal body, called the samskara, the blueprint of all our lives on Earth. It is from our past life experiences that our fate is determined. This is karma.

Carl Jung along with modern-day psychologists, place the human mind into 3 categories; First there is the Conscious Mind or the present mind. Second, the Sub-Conscious Mind, sometimes called the floating mind, and then there is the Unconscious Mind, or the buried mind. Past Life memories can be accessed through the Unconscious Mind that research shows consist of the processes in the mind which occur automatically and are not available to introspection and include thought processes, memories, interests, and motivations. Even though these thought processes exist well under the surface of conscious awareness they can affect behaviour. Research evidence shows that unconscious phenomena include regressed feelings, automatic skills, subliminal perceptions, automatic reactions and possibly also complexes, hidden phobias, and desires. The research states that the Unconscious Mind can be seen as the repository of forgotten memories. To access these memories in our samskara we need to respond to our feelings, not re-act to them. By doing this we will recall that memory, experience, and we will understand the karma, or the lessons needed to be learnt behind each experience.

Dr. Joe Dispenza has done a lot of study in quantum physics and the science of change, and states that our feelings are magnetic, so by changing our electromagnetic field we can draw to us the experiences we choose. This is cleansing the negative memories from our unconscious mind to allow for more positive experiences, memories, to be created in our energy field or samskara. The more positive our memories the more positive our life experiences will be.

According to yogis it is our feelings that create our emotions that are like the vibrating strings on a sitar, our feelings control everything that we do, and this has a karmic effect in our lives. By changing our feelings and emotional state, the whole world will change accordingly. Change the emotion, change the reality. If we feel fear, we radiate that fear to others, if we feel safe, we allow others to pick up on that energy of safety and feel safe too. If we display anger and hate, then others pick up on that energy and feel it too, consciously, or unconsciously.

Once we cultivate this energy of compassionate feelings within, all our actions will stem from compassion and this compassionate nature will free us from the cycle of birth, death, and re-birth.

Our feelings connect us to our intuitive self, they connect us to our creative self, and they activate our memories, even memories from our past lives that are embedded in the samskara, the magnetic energy field around us. Energy does not die it simply changes form.

After the Master Jesus was crucified on the cross, a couple of His disciples were travelling to Emmaus when they were joined by a 'stranger' who asked them why they were sad. They immediately began to tell the 'stranger' the news of Jesus' crucifixion, not realizing it was Jesus himself they were talking too! It was only when they sat down together to have their evening meal that they realized who this man was when He broke the bread, blessed it, and gave it to them to eat – 'and their eyes were opened, and they knew Jesus; and He vanished out of their sight.' Luke 24: 30-31.

Our experiences from past lives, and how we felt during that experience is never forgotten and can resurface at any time in this lifetime.

Jerry Lee Lewis, a musician who began a successful singing career in the 1950's said no one had to teach him anything about music because he already 'felt' all he needed to know from a young age.

And in Melbourne a girl just three years old had her paintings exhibited that showed an amazing use of colours and textures using different paintbrushes, which she changed according to her feelings.

All our memories are filed away in our mind and heart and upon death they become impressions in the Causal (subtle) body. All it takes is a feeling to recall a memory from decades ago or from another lifetime.

I remember a child in school being upset when she arrived and I asked her what was wrong and she said she was upset and sad because her little brother had broken her favourite toy, and this brought back a memory of my young brother, some 30 years before, who put my much-loved rag doll Podgy into a bucket of water and she had no face left. I could even 'feel' the sadness, and how Podgy never FELT the same even though my mother painted her a new face, with the eyes not properly lined up!

'It will go away says the time. But I'll be back, says the memory.'

The careers we choose and those we feel guided too are due to the impressions in the Causal body (Samskara). Every experience, from a life-changing moment to an interesting hobby is stored in this memory field of pure energy and it is from these impressions created by our feelings that our experiences in each lifetime are shaped.

Our likes and dislikes, our strengths and weaknesses, our talents, and hobbies, including our emotional nature is a result of how we felt during an experience, in whichever lifetime, past or present.

As adults we cannot recall every experience, we have had from the time we were a baby, yet every feeling can be remembered from our early experiences. Traumatic experiences can express themselves later in life by feeling in a negative way, like fearful, even though we cannot recall the experience that created it.

A friend of mine was afraid of driving or being driven down a hill, especially if she felt the car was going too close to the edge. She became anxious, her palms got sweaty and sometimes she even had difficulty breathing. One day she had a vision of being on a bus with school children and it went over the edge, she vividly remembered that feeling of falling and crashing but it was not from this lifetime. The memory was so strong she knew she must have experienced it in another lifetime.

Not all of us can recall an experience from the past that can explain aggressive behaviour, or feelings of being unloved, or believing, because our beliefs are connected to our feelings, we are financially poor, when we are wealthy. In a past life, we could have experienced poverty and with that a feeling of insecurity so that feeling does not want to let the money go in this lifetime, so by believing we are poor we can convince the mind it does not have enough money to purchase things, or we rationalize it by saying we do not need it when we do need it. The belief 'I do not have enough' can stay there for many lifetimes.

Our identity of who we are today is a result of the feelings we had during our experiences over many lifetimes. Plato described them as, 'mental forms imprinted in the soul and that they embodied the fundamental characteristics of a person,' and since all thought forms are created by the energy of feelings, it then translates into the Greek chi which in Eastern language refers to the life-force energy that lives on and never dies. This identity, or personality does not change with death because the human feelings of each experience, converted into energy, is contained within the soul's samskara as a memory.

My mother was very persistent when she wanted her children to do something they did not want to do and invariably she got us to do what she wanted in the end. When she died, I still felt her presence telling me what to do constantly. One day I said loudly, "Mum you are on the other side you cannot make me do it how you want it anymore!"

After that the thoughts she has sent me have been encouragingly helpful rather than pushy.

Mother Teresa of Calcutta was an extraordinary creation of her own karma because she felt compassion for the sick and dying, the disabled, the outcast, in a time when these people were abandoned. If she did not have strong feelings for the work she did, none of it would have happened. Even her beliefs were her feelings of what felt right and what did not. She said, "the right spirit is a feeling of love." Her desire to help everyone regardless of their religious beliefs and not try to make them follow her Christian belief was because she felt she had no right to do that, even though her Catholic church wanted everyone to be converted to Christianity at the time.

When I went to work as a volunteer at the Motherhouse, I felt her loving kindness everywhere I went even though she was no longer physically there.

Another remarkable woman was a German school teacher named Anna Essinger who escaped the Nazi authorities and went to live in rural England where she set up a refuge home for children from Germany, Austria, Czechoslovakia, and Poland. These remarkable women's inclusiveness, compassion and humility was far ahead of their time. These feelings came from deep within their samskara and they acted upon them in such a courageous way.

People who have learned to suppress their feelings over a long period of time can literally become unable to show feelings during any experience, good or bad. Usually, these people's feelings have been hurt over a long time so in order not to be hurt through their feelings again they suppress their feelings till eventually they feel nothing.

A man who killed 51 people in Christchurch, New Zealand told the judge at his trial that he wished he had shot more people, even after listening to his shooting of a toddler who was clinging onto his dad's leg. He was void of any feelings. The longer he suppresses his feelings the harder it will become for him to access the healing he needs to change the karma for his next life. A family member of one of the victims said to him in court "May you get the severest punishment for your evil act in this life." The experiences this murderer will need to go through in his next life will be even more painful than those he has experienced in this lifetime.

Stress in the body can make you unsure of your feelings because it is connected to the fight or flight response, two opposite forms of behaviour. If you stay in this mode for any length of time the toll it takes on the body is tremendous, just imagine your body is constantly fighting or running, even though you are not actually doing it, the mind says you are, so it stays on high alert.

Animals are much better at dealing with stress than we humans. A documentary of a lioness chasing a deer showed the deer running and jumping at top speed with the lioness close behind, it was fleeing for its life because it knew it had no chance of winning a fight with a lioness. In this case the lioness gave up the chase and the deer ran a bit further out of harm's way and found a nice patch of grass and started happily eating swishing her tail with content. The deer instantly let go of the fear and anxiety because the danger had passed.

And recently a 3-year-old little boy named Jimmy got lost in the bush and was missing for twelve hours. When he was found by his distraught grandfather he said, "I was bit tired, and I gone to bed." Completely lost and alone, he chose the best option to release stress by finding a place to lie down and go to sleep.

Most people, on the other hand, hold onto that fear and anxiety during and after the experience, thereby creating more fearful, anxious cells in the body.

Here is a simple de-stressing exercise to have a 'feel good' experience -

Place your hand over your heart space and close your eyes and FEEL the calmness by silently saying, calm, calm, calm, and as you are breathing imagine the breath is coming in and out of your heart.

Being truthful with your feelings is paramount in cultivating good karma for this life and the next. This is most difficult to do because most of us do not want to hurt other people's feelings, but the truth of your own feelings, overrides being untruthful to others. The evolution of the human mind to higher levels of consciousness is when we start living a life of truth.

There is a story of a teacher teaching her young student's subtraction, she said, "A farmer had 12 sheep, 6 of the sheep jumped the fence and ran away, how many sheep did the farmer have left?"

A little boy said "Six" and the teacher praised him for giving the correct answer. But another little boy, who lived on a farm, raised his hand, and said, "None would be left Miss, because I knows the way of sheep."

Here we see the Truth being revealed in a very different way.

Jeff Brown in his book, Ascending with Both Feet on the Ground, explains Truth like this "I imagine Truth, as a magnificent, white-tipped Mountain. At its peak is a deeper and more inclusive experience of the moment. As we move through our lives, Truth Mountain comes in and out of view, calling out to us and reminding us of what is possible. The more truthful we are about our path, the higher our consciousness climbs. When our view is blocked, we know that we still have work to do in the valleys down below traversing the foothills of illusion, sidestepping the quick sands of artifice, overcoming our fear of (interior) heights. But we will get to the peak, if we are willing to do the work, if we can be truthful with ourselves about the ways we avoid the truth."

This behaviour of avoiding the truth can be seen even in very young children.

A priest was taking a Sunday school class of 5-year-old children, and he asked one boy, "Do you say your prayers every night?"

The boy said, "No Father because some nights I don't want anything."

So, the priest explained the importance of praying for others, even for the birds and animals and plants not just for oneself. The next day a little girl from that class told her mother that she had prayed to God to send snow because she really wanted to go out and play in the snow, but she told God to "Please send the beautiful snow to keep the plants warm."

When we tell the Truth our story changes; when our story changes our life is transformed. We are the story tellers, not the story.

The Master Jesus said, "I Am the Way, the Truth and the Life." (St.

John's Gospel 14:6) And in John 8:32 Jesus said, "Then you will know the Truth, and the Truth will set you free."

This Truth is the Light of enlightenment, the freedom from all negative karma collected over many, many lifetimes; and it is the only way we can be set free from the cycle of birth, death, and rebirth. It is the gift of good karma, like reward points for our next life. But it can only come through our feelings. We do not just speak the Truth we must feel passionate about it too. This Truth must become our reality because we cannot be in the Real if we are not emotionally Real.

Truth develops into Trust which allows us to experience Love. Truth, Trust, and Love are one when there is authenticity. Some people speak untruths like a joke, but they are usually hiding a deeper truth via fear within, to avoid showing their true feelings.

Alcohol and drugs hinder us from truthfully expressing our feelings. When one is under the influence of either of them one's feelings get distorted, and it is hard to know whether what you are feeling is real or not and the longer one stays holding onto these distorted feelings the possibility of one accepting them as real becomes stronger. This becomes a trap of never being sure of one's feelings. The experiences from here on are usually painful and disappointing. This is most noticeable in relationships, which feelings are real, and which are not? Conflicting feelings cause a relationship to break up and you could miss finding your soulmate, which is one of the most fulfilling experiences one can have in a lifetime. This does not mean that life is perfect with a soul mate, it is karma being acted upon and is for the evolution of two souls to a higher level of consciousness. Sometimes harsh lessons need to be learned that they need to do together.

My husband Ken said it was love at first sight when he saw me, his feelings were so strong because it was also a recollection from a past life. It was our True-Path that needed to be taken in this lifetime.

For Michael Newton, author of Journey of Souls, love at first sight is 'the light of spiritual identity being reflected in the human eyes of a soulmate.' And he also said 'I have knowingly experienced this instant recognition only once in my life, the moment I first saw my own wife. The effect is startling, and a bit eerie as well.'

Another woman told me her husband first saw her in a photo and told people that was the girl he was going to marry; he was from Australia, and she was in Scotland they met and got married and have been together for many years.

Then there is the story of Georgina Wilkins who was born in the Northam hospital in Western Australia during the war years, and due to a shortage of baby cots was placed in a cot with baby Eric Lawrence, who had been born three days earlier. At the age of 18 she joined the Royal Australian Air Force and went to live in South Australia. On a visit back to Northam she met up with Eric Lawrence and they married in 1947. They were married for 75 years until her death in 2022.

Relationships are the most vital part of our lives whether they are family or friends or workmates and the more familiar they feel to us the chances that they were connected to us from a past life are highly probable. These people are important to us because they need to learn something from us, and we need to learn something from them.

When my son was seventeen years old, he was involved in a horrific car accident, in which his friend Alex who was the driver of the car was killed. Alex's parents suffered the deepest grief anyone could suffer, the pain would just not go away.

One day I sat talking to Tim, Alex's father, and he told me he always felt Alex was going to leave him whilst he was still young. He said that in a past life he had been Alex's son, and he had committed suicide at a young age and Alex, in that previous life, never got over the pain of losing him, Tim, so tragically. Now in this life Tim was experiencing that same heartbreaking pain of losing a beloved son.

Our karmic experiences will keep giving us those experiences that allow us to fully feel how we make others feel in this journey of life.

People who commit suicide do not understand how their loved ones will feel by their act of suicide. Their feelings of hopelessness and helplessness are so strong it consumes them to the point where they believe those are the only feelings they will ever have, and they block feelings of their loved ones out and become emotionally detached. They keep creating new cells in their body that have these same negative feelings and eventually the feeling of hopelessness becomes so strong they give up. Unfortunately, in their next life they will have to work through those same feelings to release that karma that caused so much pain to others. They will have to experience heartache and pain to release that karma.

Our life is not about survival but about living a life of authenticity. Swami Umeshranand explained it to me like this-

We are each born with 3 modes of Samskara; Sattva Guna represents the goodness already within us. Rajas Guna means the level of greed and desire within the samskara; and Tamas Guna is the level of ignorance in our memory. This ignorance is the mind refusing to accept the Truth over many lifetimes.

Our Karma depends on the level of Guna in the Samskara at each lifetime. For example, if Sattva is at 60%, we will do good in the world and live a successful life.

On the other hand, for those people where 80% of Rajas Guna is in the Samskara the greed for more power or material wealth will be so overwhelming, they will take the path of attaining that no matter what the cost to themselves or others. Taking another path to this one would be difficult because they will be going against their nature that is implanted in their samskara.

Likewise, if Tamas Guna is 80% then there is a lot of catching up on wisdom to do in this lifetime. My mother used to refer to people who refused to accept good advice as stubbornness. In truth it was a carry on of their nature from past lives.

The Hindu holy book, Bhagavad Gita explains this law of karma in 3: 27 – 'The bewildered soul under the influence of the three modes of Guna thinks itself to be the doer of activities that are being carried out by nature.'

My mother-in-law used to refer to people who said they would do something but never did as 'Guna' people. Perhaps there was some truth in it!

To get a better understanding of the three Guna's and how they interact with our mind in the physical body via the auric field and nadis, we need to look at these pictures to help understand the Soul body that is a permanent part of us lifetime after lifetime.

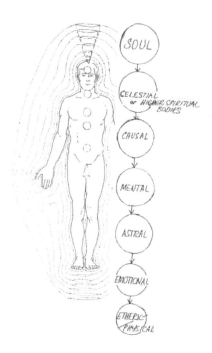

The Subtle Bodies are interactive, multidimensional bands of energy that resonate at frequencies according to the consciousness or 'openness' of the individual. They connect via the chakras, nadis and samskara (auric field). Often referred to as the Celestial Layer, it extends beyond the physical body and connects via the Pituitary Gland. It is the level of Spiritual Essence and is of an extremely high frequency where the individual reaches a point of 'being' and knows his/her connection with all the Universe. It can be reached through meditation and transformational yoga. When we align with higher vibrations, we tap into powerful subatomic energy around us and this facilitates intentional healing. (I will include a program for Samanvaya yoga at the end of this book.)

Each of us contains all the memories of our past lives in our Samskara, referred to today as the Bio-field or electromagnetic field, or auric field, located about 10 inches outside the body. Sadhguru refers to this as the 'Akashic dimension around your body.' (Inner Engineering pg.179).

This energy space stores the memories of all our lives, past and present, that hold tremendous influence on our health and well-being, memories of unresolved issues to hidden gifts. This energy space holds the memories of pain, struggles, and passed along patterns, as well as the blessings of our past lives – traits and talents that lie latent within. Many of our personal challenges, traumas, fear, stress, depression, anxiety, issues of self-worth, lack of purpose, unfulfilled desires, hopes, and dreams are unresolved issues from our past lives.

These memories impact and limit us, and affect our relationships between siblings, parents, and partners. These past life memories distort our present life experiences due to the 'passed on' pattern of behaviours linked to those in our memory field, samskara.

What we think is what we create because our thoughts are created from our memories and our memories are created from our experiences. So, if we had a bad experience with dogs our thoughts about dogs stay locked in with that bad past life experience with dogs. Knowing and understanding past lives helps us to live in the now by responding to what is, instead of re-acting to what was a past life experience/memory that will constantly sabotage us. Past life memories distort our present life experiences and hold us back, like an invisible force, from reaching our full potential because our strongest memories are from our most traumatic experiences, the ones that carry the heaviest emotions/feelings.

Knowing a past life memory is liberating because we understand what has been holding us back from going forward in this lifetime. It also stops us from looking for someone or something to blame for our current situation. All painful memories from past lives can be transformed when we know where those memories came from, sometimes going through a past life experience can be very painful because the conscious mind must re-live that experience and replace it with a memory of healing and forgiveness, for your past life self or for someone else. This will bring resolution to that past problem so that this current life can be celebrated more consciously. When the conscious mind re-lives a past life experience it allows the image of that memory to heal, and re-generate at a cellular level within the body, through a new awareness.

None of us are losers, we are all high achievers, that's what we have been designed for and that is why we returned to this lifetime; so, let your current life reflect that.

The Soul body is the seventh layer of the aura. It is that part of our sub molecular SELF that holds the spark of the I AM ALL THAT IS.

The 13th century Persian poet Rumi said, "I AM a spiritual being; I know who I AM; I know why I AM here."

And this about the Soul body from the great Indian poet Kabir –

"I live in it; it lives in me.

The one who knows it never dies,

The one who doesn't know it dies again and again."

Together with the chakras, the nadis are part of the subtle body. These nerve-like conduits constitute channels of the flow of subtle vital energy known as prana, the universal pure energy that we can draw into our body when we practice pranayama, deep controlled breathing.

James Bailey, who was a student of Kabir once asked him 'Where is God?' His answer was "He is the breath within the breath."

In the next illustration you will see the extent of the nerves radiating beyond the outer body into the samskara. Hundreds of years ago yogis knew about the biofield of magnetic and radiant energy the nerves create that act as an internal feedback system of our physical and spiritual nature. Our connection to each other is physical, emotional, and spiritual and this inner knowing comes via the nerves, often referred to as the spiritual nexus. Science today is confirming the connection between consciousness and the biofield and the whole person healing through this subtle energy.

The Vagus Nerve, that is connected to our crown chakra, when aroused can retrieve latent intelligence from our past lives that can shift the entire physiology of our personality and behaviour. This inner knowing then helps us to become better choice makers. The Vagus Nerve plays a vital role in supporting our innate intelligence and overall spiritual development. It's central to the spiritual nexus that connects the body/mind to our spirit consciousness and is the only nerve that connects our human physical nature with our spiritual nature via the kundalini energy.

At the base of our spine is a nerve called Medha Nadi. This nerve lies dormant throughout most people's lives but can be activated through deep levels of meditation and celibacy. This is why celibacy is practiced among spiritual masters because sexual energy blocks this nerve, medha nadi, from raising upwards and connecting with the vagus nerve. The rising of the Kundalini energy is the awakening of considerable spiritual powers.

According to Swami Brahmananda when these two nerves connect, Vagus and Medha Nadi, we enjoy bodily health, peace of mind, and spiritual joy.

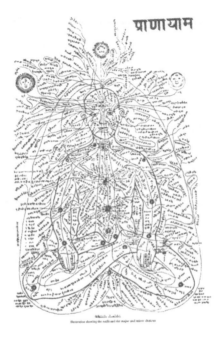

The idea of the nadis first appeared in the Hindu sacred book The Upanishads around the 7th century B.C.E. The heart was believed to be able to connect to all these nadis, 72,000 of them via the Sushumna channel in the spinal cord and the two largest nadis in the back, Ida and Pingala. Ida being the feminine energy, connected to the moon and Pingala being male energy connected to the sun. When these energies are flowing freely the human mind can be transformed and purified through the third eye, called the Ajna chakra, into the Guna's. This part of the human brain, the cerebral cortex, that is connected to our thoughts and personality is closest to the third eye. When this area of our mind is transformed, to a higher level of thinking and consciousness, that some refer to as cognitive restructuring, the levels of Rajas and Tamas Guna drop and Sattva Guna, the goodness that is within us is enhanced, thereby erasing the negative karma from previous lifetimes and this current lifetime from the samskara.

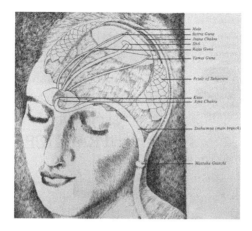

This illustration clearly shows where the Guna's are in the human brain, even though they cannot be proved medically yet. But we do know that the Hippocampus, situated at the edge of the cortex in the limbic system of the brain, manages the functions of feelings and re-acting, and retrieves memory. It was medically discovered by Surgeon Julius Caesar Arantius in 1587. He also discovered that short term memories are converted into long term memories in the Hippocampus, and now medical science is telling us that memories are also stored in other parts of the body, in the gut and heart. Yet yogis had this information from the 7th century and believed that all our memories were stored in the samskara and returned into our new brain each lifetime via the Guna's.

Shri Prabhupada said, "Whatever one aspires to in this life will determine the type of body they get in their next. The ultimate perfection in human life is the development of consciousness. Human beings can transmigrate to either a higher or lower form of life; those endowed with discretion receive a higher human form. Lack of awareness is ignorance, when our light is dim our consciousness is material."

Karmic debt has an ethical educative purpose, it is not about punishment.

The sayings, what goes around comes around, and as you sow so shall you reap, refer to the learning experiences in life whether they are painful or joyful. Life takes us from smooth sailing to stormy seas, if we hang onto that feeling of being blessed in whatever way we can find, we will sail through all our challenges.

Shri Prabhupada said "No one can become perfect through imperfect feelings. Darkness does not produce light."

The more power you give negative feelings, the more chances there are of them becoming your reality, because you believe them, and a belief is a thought that you keep thinking. Our feelings are connected to our senses, so if you see life as the glass half full, instead of half empty, you will always be in a place of gratitude for what you have in life instead of what is missing from your life.

Do this simple exercise:

Relax your whole body. Now sitting with your spine tall and straight take a deep breath in; and as you exhale say, 'All is well with me.' Now take a normal breath in and out, now repeat the deep breath in and as you exhale say, 'all is well with me.' Do this simple exercise 3x and you will notice a shift in your feelings to feeling more blessed and grateful as your feelings flow with acceptance.

My time spent with Swami Umeshranand at Yoga Niketan Ashram in Rishikesh, India was an experience of being blessed to listen to the wisdom of an enlightened being in today's world.

The first thing he requested I do was become a vegetarian. At that time there were not many Christian vegetarians, and I did not want to become one of the first, besides Jesus ate meat and I enjoyed eating meat. Swami ji said, 'You are not Jesus the Christ, and it has nothing to do with religion, meat disturbs the fine balance between the peaceful Self and the aggressive Self, if you want to do spiritual work you need to stay in the peaceful mind."

I returned to Perth and continued with my meat diet. About two months later I awoke from a deep sleep and saw the most beautiful, serene figure at the end of the bed – a goddess flashed through my conscious mind – I said, "Who are you?" via my thoughts.

She said, to my mind, "I AM Shakti, and I will help you become a vegetarian."

And she was gone.

I have been a vegetarian for over 30 years, and I do believe I feel more balanced and calmer due to my diet of fruit and vegetables, and other non- meat foods. I think of the dinosaurs, the largest one Brontosaurus was a gentle plant eating giant whereas Tyrannosaurus Rex was a ferocious predator.

I also felt good that I had taken the advice of my mentor, as I believe the beautiful Goddess Shakti helped me, like she said she would.

Spiritual growth does not mean a laborious journey on your own. Swami ji used to tell us, "When the student is ready the Master will appear, but the pupil needs a teacher whose wisdom is within his or her grasp. The teacher should, therefore, be only a few rungs further up the ladder than the pupil."

'You cannot choose a Guru. Deepen your longing and the Guru will choose you.' Sadhguru.

In the Guru yoga practice saying this mantra with devotion will connect one to the mind of their guru or master: Om Ah Hum Vajra Guru Padma Siddhi Hum.

In my own journey of developing the conscious mind I have found help through books, teachers, gurus, friends, yoga, my church, the list is endless. Once you consciously make the effort the right help will come to you from all directions. The biggest challenge is being able to embrace the Truth because sometimes it will mean letting go of old beliefs that do not ring true for us anymore. Like re-incarnation, where my own beliefs were challenged because as a Christian I did not believe in re-incarnation. When I was young, I believed dead people stayed in their graves till Jesus came again and set them free. But I did wonder why God kept making more and more new Souls each time a baby was born. Now I know that the Souls are simply re-cycled!

Swami Umeshranand explained to me the process of birth (Barth), death and re-birth.

'The consciousness of the samskara arises from one's mind in each lifetime. When the mind dissolves in death all the memory is retained within the samskara, as energy in the auric field, which then feeds these previous memories back into the re-birth mind as it expands with new memories in the next life.

When the mind dissolves, after it has transferred all memory into the samskara, the body dies. Each new body develops from the mind and our existence is molded by the five elements of earth, water, fire, air, and ether that are within the mind. The link between the mind and the 5 elements are like this:

The mind is the ground, Earth, where all our experiences are planted.
It is active and adaptive like water.
The element of fire gives the mind the ability to perceive things clearly.
It moves from one thing to another like air.
It is boundless, formless, and empty like space (ether).
These five elements are within us and around us in each lifetime.'

Our samskara holds all our memories, feelings, from each lifetime, so depending on how we FELT during each experience our perception, intellect and consciousness of our mind will be influenced by those feelings.

Swami Umeshranand explained death to me, "When death approaches the elements exit the mind in the following manner; first the mind experiences drowsiness and as it moves deeper the feeling of being grounded goes and the element of Earth moves out and the mind reverts back to the fetal stage of being immersed in water, as the water dries up the mind becomes aware of sparks of light in a smoky haze, then as the fire element dissolves the mind finds it almost impossible to perceive anything on the outside anymore as it envisions wisps of white haze float away as air moves out of the body.

With the element of air out of the mind all contact with the physical world slips away, and finally there is a feeling of being consumed by the entire Universe, with visions according to one's karma –meeting enlightened beings and loving family and friends are felt by those with a compassionate mind, whilst a negative mind will feel fear and separation."

Each lifetime we are here to learn by different experiences through our feelings that includes our interaction with people, animals, plants, and everything that this Earth provides, consciously and unconsciously.

The Buddha said, "A lifetime is like a flash of lightening in the sky. Like a rushing torrent down a steep mountain."

The book of Psalms (90:4) puts it like this, 'For a thousand years in your sight are like yesterday passing, or like one watch of the night.'

Our time here, factual time, is short, even though in our linear time on earth it appears longer. In the afterlife the time we get to spend on earth is not long at all so we need to do as much good as we can in whatever time we have here to create good karma because our past lives impact on our present life in many ways.

The more we understand this process of our existence on Earth and the purpose of it all, which is to serve, we will live and die in peace because this memory will be firmly embedded in the samskara. Our negative feelings come from fear and the uncertainty of what the purpose of our life is. All service is honourable when it is done for the good of all humanity, but more often than not we are more concerned in how we serve than in the service itself and this comes via our big dreams for ourself and the experiences we wish to create for ourself, then how we feel doing that service becomes distorted, because we believe the bigger the dream the bigger the experience and the happier we will feel.

This lovely children's story perfectly shows how karmic bondage, big dreams, can be transformed into karmic liberation, humble service.

Once upon a time three trees stood tall and beautiful in a forest on a mountaintop. The first tree had dreams of grandeur and said he wanted to be a treasure chest with intricate carvings done on the lid, perfectly varnished, and polished and filled with gold and silver and precious jewels. The second tree dreamt of adventure and said he wanted to be a mighty sailing ship that would travel the oceans of Earth taking Kings and important people to distant lands. The third tree wanted to remain a tree, standing high and tall on the mountain top for all to see and admire.

That summer the woodcutters arrived, and the first tree was chopped down and taken to a carpenter's shop. This tree was sure he was going to be made into a beautiful chest, but instead he was made into a feed box for animals. Instead of being filled with treasure animals came and slobbered all over him while they ate their food!

The second tree couldn't believe his luck when he was taken to a shipbuilding yard, but instead of being transformed into a mighty sailing ship he was made into a simple fishing boat and taken out to a lake where fishermen filled him with smelly fish every day.

The third tree was confused when she was cut down and taken to a lumberyard and thrown onto a pile of logs. 'Why did they chop me down?' she thought 'all I wanted was to stay high up on the mountain for all to see.'

Time passed, then one night the feed box was cleaned out and fresh hay placed inside, and a newborn baby was placed into the feed box. As the first tree felt the warmth of the new baby and heard the rhythm of the baby's breath the tree knew he was holding the greatest treasure on Earth, his wish had come true in a way he could never have imagined.

One day the fishing boat, whilst sitting in the middle of the lake was suddenly tossed about by a raging storm. The second tree felt powerless and knew he could not stay upright for much longer. Then a voice said "Peace" and the raging storm stopped, and a calmness descended on the lake like the fishing boat had never experienced before; then the fishing boat felt his wooden frame expand into a 'mighty sailing ship' as he felt a new power within him.

Very early one morning, after many years of lying on a wood pile in the lumberyard the third tree was yanked from the wood pile, roughly cut into two lengths, and carried by a man through the city with a hostile mob of people following. She shuddered as a man was nailed into her. She stood there, tall, and still, and then the Heavens appeared to open, and light streamed down upon her, and she knew her symbol, the cross, would forever be recognized as a sacred symbol on Earth.

Sometimes our dreams are too big for our minds to contain so we imagine the trappings of life, glorifying them with our ego. Then reality strikes, karma plays its hand, the ego takes a beating, and we are left with an experience, a memory, so profound it transforms our body, mind, and Soul through our humble service. This service comes from a place of unconditional kindness, when we are no longer motivated to do good through sensory gratification or self-interest, instead our involvement is inclusive and based on the needs of others. This attitude of ours comes from our higher Self that is beyond our senses. The world of the senses is motivated by external stimuli and takes us away from following our true path of sacred service. It is only when we can transform and transcend these sensory instincts can we gain liberation from the karmic wheel of suffering.

In the Bhagavad Gita (11: 14-15)

'The world of the senses gives rise to heat and cold, pleasure and pain.

They come and they go and do not last. Bear them patiently.

For a person unmoved by these changes, for whom sorrow, and happiness is the same,

is truly wise and fit for immortality.'

Bhagavad Gita (11:58)
'Even as the tortoise withdraws all its limbs,
The wise can draw in their senses at will.'

Someone who comes to this lifetime with high levels of Rajas Guna, greed, and desire, might appear to have it all in the beginning, but it often all comes crashing down later in their life due to karmic justice. The story of Boris Becker is an example. He was a tennis legend beginning with winning the men's Wimbledon at just 17 years of age that allowed him to live a lavish lifestyle of greed that enabled him to satisfy his every desire. He was finally sent to jail for owing his creditors almost $90 million. When sentencing him the judge condemned his lack of remorse or humility and told him he was the 'architect of his own downfall' but for people with high levels of Rajas Guna it is part of their nature of who they are, and that is why they cannot comprehend that there is anything wrong with their behaviour.

On the other hand, people who have come to Earth with high levels of Sattva Guna are able to feel and act beyond their senses. Mother Teresa of Calcutta was such a person. When she decided to leave her good paying job as a school principal at a prestigious girl's school and build a home for unwanted children, her first need was to find a suitable home for the children to live in, but she soon found that with her limited funds she could not afford to buy anything with the money she had.

Requests for money to Governments and wealthy businesses only fell on deaf ears so in desperation she decided to go 'begging.' One day whilst begging she approached a well-dressed man and stretched out her hand and asked if he could spare a few coins to help her care for homeless children. The man spat in her hand! Without the slightest display of emotion, she put that hand behind her back and stretched out her other hand and said, "that hand was for me, now this hand is for the children."

The man was so shocked he became one of her biggest financial supporters. The nuns, women, who worked with her often spoke of her ability to work for long periods of time without feeling hungry or thirsty, or cold or hot, or even showing signs of tiredness. Sometimes they had to remind her to eat or put on warmer clothing if the weather got cooler. Her service to others was so focused that her own needs, via her senses, were not felt by her. Pratyahara, the withdrawal of the senses in yoga, was part of her everyday life due to her high levels of Sattva Guna.

Recently a woman named Danica Joysdottir left her safe comfortable home in Perth, Western Australia where she lived with her partner and four-year-old son to travel to Ukraine as a volunteer paramedic to help the people who were suffering due to the war with Russia. Her only comment from the war zone was, "the outpouring of generosity from the Polish people is humbling to me." No comment on the hardships or suffering she might have been experiencing, just the kindness and goodness of others.

This comes with the practice of pratyahara, when our own needs take a back seat, and the needs of others take prominence in our mind. This transformation of the mind leads to the destruction of all karma and to enlightenment, where there is only GOODNESS in the unconscious mind, in the subconscious mind, and in the super conscious mind. This is the purity of the samskara.

"Who is wise? He who learns from everyone.
Who is powerful? He that governs his passions.
Who is rich? He that is content." Benjamin Franklin 1776

Today there is a lot of research being done in epigenetics that connects our physical and emotional behaviour to our DNA which is in our genes that we inherit from our parents. It is the belief that our behaviour relates to our ancestral imprints, whereby our physical traits and predispositions have been passed down through the generations of our family, especially significant events that happened in our ancestors' lives. The study states that the code of ethics people live by, their sense of purpose, their relationship to money, and how they relate to success, failure, and the people who come into their life, are in their genetic make-up. The study endorses the idea that our behaviour is encoded in our genes which we will then pass on to future generations.

According to a study epigenetic changes do not affect DNA sequences, but they can impact how the body 'reads' DNA sequences, and thereby alter gene expression according to environmental and psychosocial factors that trigger on some genes and switch others off.

This kind of research excludes the presence of subtle energies found in the samskara that are passed on lifetime after lifetime via the gunas and can be seen in siblings who are very different to the rest of their family members, whereby one child can be utterly selfish in a family by always demanding they get more, a case of its all about me, whilst another child in the same family just gives unselfishly. For each child it is part of their physical nature and predispositions as they are simply following their innate nature. The child with the higher levels of Sattva Guna will naturally respond and behave differently to the child with higher levels of Rajas Guna.

According to yogis, children who choose parents who will help them to consider others through service (karma yoga) will help them the most on their journey towards enlightenment.

Hindus and Buddhists call it Dharma, serving with ethical behaviour, making the right choice while serving oneself and others. Dharma is living a good life with intentional right action that allows us to just BE our peaceful self even when life is a drama of chaos, uncertainty, and challenges. Learn to trust your feelings when you serve because we usually do work that is already in our memory from another lifetime.

May Gibbs, a famous Australian artist and writer said, "I could draw almost as soon as I could walk. I loved drawing." Some of her most famous works, the Gumnut Babies, and Snugglepot and Cuddlepie are still read by children, and adults, today.

Kylee Legge who was two years old at the time and could neither read nor write, told her grandmother a story she called 'Nana went fishing.' The book got published and sold many thousand copies.

My own son also used to make-up interesting stories from the age of two, my husband even recorded one story on a tape because we thought it was so good. Unfortunately, that tape got lost. Today my son is a published author.

I read a story of a woman who had a beautiful singing voice. People who heard her singing in church asked her to join the choir. She refused saying she was too embarrassed, even at school she would not sing at any of the school performances. But she sang at home and her family were always enthralled by her beautiful voice. When she got older, she experienced a past life, and she was able to re-call a memory of being an attractive Jewish girl working in the kitchens in a concentration camp.

One day an officer heard her singing in the kitchen, and he took her to sing for the other officers, after singing to them he took her back to the kitchen and raped her. This soon became a regular occurrence, that lead to her being abused by the other officers too. The feeling of shame became so unbearable she ended her life in that past life.

After this past life experience in therapy, she went on to sing at large concerts and said that when she sang her spirit felt free. That past life memory brought healing to her in this lifetime and the gift, hidden within the pain, was released.

Past life therapy has shown that the gift found in our healing will be past life talents and abilities. We often must let go of any fear or disappointment we suffered in the past before the gift can be restored to us in a useful way this lifetime.

Dr. Roger Woolger, a past life therapist and a Jungian analyst says life is a continuity of consciousness. He believes that past life memories can and do affect the quality of our life experiences in this current life.

A friend of mine teaches young children and is dedicated to her job and the children in her care. She goes way beyond the call of duty in her devotion to them, each class of children she taught became her kids. But from young she told her mother she never wanted to be a mother. Before her marriage she told her husband- to- be she would not have children with him and he accepted that, yet she loved children. At a psychic- medium session she was told that in her past life she had had six children who had all been sexually abused by their father, her husband. She left with her children and had to work as a prostitute. She felt betrayed and hurt in that lifetime. In this lifetime that memory must have come back to her, as a little girl, when she told her mother that she never wanted to have children and be a mother.

Past life memories not only help us to deal with life they also help us to deal with death. Having my own past life experience with Ken has helped me deal with his death in a very accepting way because I know that our separation is only physical. Our love for each other was unconditional and that feeling of love has not changed by his death.

In 1957 a school friend wrote these words in my autograph book, 'To be loved by the one you love is the greatest gift of all.' Staying grateful for that gift of love that I shared with Ken was a stronger feeling than the feeling of grief and physical separation. Death cannot separate love, it is eternal.

One of my yoga students, Caroline, gave me a picture she had done called Eternal Heart. It is of a dying flower, gerbera, yet the yellow colour of the stamens shaped like a heart in the center kept getting brighter and brighter whilst the flower was dying.

My reading at Ken's funeral strengthened my belief that we could never be spiritually separated. I felt him saying these words to me even though he was not there in physical form. It felt as if he was saying the words through me.

"Beloved here I AM and there you are,
We are inextricably woven by our unique human threads,
With and of and in this whole tapestry of infinite creation.
Beloved I am fading, happily fading,
Soon I am not sure I will have anything more to say-
There will only be love in all its manifestations.
Will you join me Beloved?
We cannot meet in the middle because the middle does not exist.
Lets' meet everywhere--------
For wherever you are – there I AM."

Whilst reading these words at his funeral I could also feel the comfort of the Master Jesus' words, "Lo I Am with you always, even unto the end." (Matthew28:20)

Lord Buddha referred to deaths' certainty for all of us when he said, "This existence of ours is as transient as autumn clouds. To watch the birth and death of human beings is like looking at the movements of a dance."

Once we understand this process of life, death, and re-birth we can let our loved ones go with feelings of love and gratitude, not by feeling abandoned or feeling the emotion of guilt or fear of the unknown. We can accept death without becoming overwhelmed by the grief.

'We do not need to grieve for the dead. Why should we grieve for them? They are now in a place where there is no more shadow, darkness, loneliness, isolation, or pain. They are home.' John O'Donohue, Anam Cara

This is true, but it is not possible not to grieve after the loss of someone special from our life because physical separation is painful and hard to deal with. Even after time the loss can be overwhelming and can overcome one like waves or shadows of variable intensity. If unmanaged it can provoke anger or agitation, and even provide triggers for mental illness that can lead into depression. And if we add to this past life experiences of grief and the karma connected to it, the memories of suppressed and unresolved trauma escalates significantly and the ability to function normally with everyday life becomes impossible, because each death experience can be an opening for another death experience from a past life to enter our current experience of death.

Recently there was a big story in the U.S. of a prominent lawyer in South Carolina who murdered his wife and son. He was given three life sentences for his crimes. The second son, Buster, who was away at the time of the murders must go down this path of grief and loss of his mother, brother, and deal with the horrendous truth of his father's actions and imprisonment and move on with living his life. The memories that he will hold in his samskara from these terrible experiences will re-occur in his next life, and perhaps in other lifetimes too.

Frank Prentice was a young boy who was rescued on a cold black night in the Atlantic Ocean when the Titanic sank. At the age of 90 years re-telling that story caused him to break down due to the trauma he had suffered by that experience because the memory was still so strong within him, and he will carry it with him forever into the next life and the next until they are resolved. By giving our painful memories less power, we can live in the now more joyfully but silencing them will not bring healing.

When we accept re-incarnation as a truth and see life as life-death-re-birth, the actual death experience, whether peaceful or traumatic, depending on the karmic implications, will hold no power over us; it will just be an experience that opens the door to more service and more experiences.

Albert Einstein said after his friend Michele Besso died, 'Now Besso has departed from this strange world a little ahead of me. That means nothing. People like us know that the distinction between past, present, and future is only a stubbornly persistent illusion.'

Today modern physics is even questioning whether death exists. Biocentrism proports the notion that death cannot exist in any real sense because all possible Universe's exist simultaneously. Although we shed our bodies, our energy lives on.

'One of the absolutes of science is that energy can neither be created nor destroyed consequently the energy associated with our identity doesn't disappear at death.' (Lanza 2009)

Our Identity is made up of our experiences, therefore our memories, and because most of our memories are from our past lives, means that they are not only stored in our brain that is discarded at death but in our energy field that makes up our Soul energy, and now neurosurgeons are validating this belief too.

Dr. Eben Alexander, a highly successful neurosurgeon, suffered his own neurological crisis when his brain became infected with E. coli bacteria that destroyed his neocortex, the part of the brain that holds memory and conscious thought. It was reduced to a lump of pus. After his long illness and slow recovery what baffled him and his colleagues the most was that all Dr. Alexanders memories, or life history returned, leaving only one possible answer, memories are stored elsewhere and can be 'downloaded' back into the brain later. This supports the belief that all our memories are stored in the samskara and can be remembered by the mind at any given time in our life.

Some years ago, I had a young woman Debbie, not her real name, come to my yoga class and during the relaxation session at the end I 'saw' a little child, around 18 months old, dancing around Debbie. She had on a white smocked dress, and she looked happy. When the yoga class ended another student approached me and said when she opened her eyes after the relaxation session, she 'thought' she saw a small child nearby, and I said I saw her too. Debbie overheard us and came over and obviously very destressed said, "what are you talking about" I said it was nothing to be concerned about Marcy and I had seen a happy little 'spirit' girl skipping around her during the relaxation session. Debbie started crying and I could feel her pain and sadness, she told us a few months earlier her baby girl had drowned in the bath. Debbie had answered the phone and when she returned to the bathroom the little girl was face down in the water, she grabbed her out and did CPR whilst waiting for the ambulance to arrive, but it was too late for her little girl was gone. Debbie told me she dressed her baby in a smocked white nightie that she was going to put on her after her bath.

Debbie started doing yoga to try and help her deal with her sadness and enormous feelings of guilt. This kind of guilt makes the whole grieving process much harder to bear because the memory connected to the feeling of loss is so intense because there is blame towards herself – 'I am responsible for my child's death.'

The karmic attachment to this experience can be dissolved only when Debbie forgives herself; it is a lesson in self-forgiveness, otherwise this karmic experience in her energy field will continue to give her painful and harsh experiences again and again until she finds the peace in self-forgiveness.

I met a young couple whose baby died in a hot car. Mum normally dropped her off at day-care in the mornings but on this occasion, Dad was to do that job, but he drove to his office and forgot the child sleeping in her baby capsule at the back. Some hours later he got a phone call and rushed to his car, but it was too late, their baby could not be saved.

Years later they had another baby who was born without a stomach and other severe disabilities who needed constant care. They devoted their life to caring for her full-time and could not let her out of their sight. Both parents were given a karmic lesson in self- sacrifice and atonement for their past mistake.

In the Christian Bible (John 9: 1-3) reference is made by Jesus' disciples to karma when they saw a man who had been blind since birth and they asked Jesus, "Who sinned he or his parents, that he was born blind?" Jesus said, "neither." The fact that the disciples asked if a newborn baby had sinned is a reference to karma.

Yogis say that all our actions whether intentional or unintentional have karmic connections. But this does not mean that all people with disabilities have them because of past wrongdoing; it could be because they want to contribute more to humankind through service because their disability heightens their feelings, they have more empathy for others and their mind becomes stronger as it focuses on specific solutions to life's problems.

Stephen Hawkins suffered from the debilitating motor neuron disease for more than 50 years, yet he made an amazing contribution to science through his interpretation of cosmological observations and gravitational wave detectors.

Each lifetime gives us the opportunity to offer greater service through more love, wisdom, gratitude, and respect, which stem from our feelings. People who cope with the challenges of life with a disability often have these virtues stronger in their personality which allows them to attain a higher level of consciousness because of their disability.

Prof. Earnest Wood spent time in an Ashram in India that was owned and run by a blind yogi. The yogi told Prof. Wood that in his past life he had come with a high percentage of Rajas Guna, and from his position of authority he had been very abusive and cruel to the people under him. He said, "I choose to be born blind in this life so I could have a nobler nature."

Our purpose for being here is to serve. Samurai, the name given to the Japanese warriors, means 'those who serve,' a service that demanded total loyalty, bravery, and honour. In the Hindu Holy Book, The Bhagavad Gita Lord Krishna tells Arjun, a soldier, 'A warrior is someone who faces their battles without any bitterness.'

Arjun was a soldier fighting for his King, a job he truly despised yet here he was again off to fight the battle of Mahabharata. The whole notion of war, the killing, the destruction of people's lives and the pain and suffering war caused brought immense sorrow to his soul, but duty had brought him once again in his chariot heading out for another battle, but this time his charioteer is Lord Krishna. Here he pours out his heart to Lord Krishna.

Bhagavad Gita 1: 28,29,31,47: 'O Krishna my limbs are giving way, and my mouth is drying up. My whole body shudders. My mind is whirling in confusion. I do not see how any good can come from killing in this battle. I do not wish to slay them, even if they attack me.' In 2:5 Arjun tells Lord Krishna, 'I would rather live a life of begging than of killing.' 'Speaking thus Arjun cast aside his bow and arrows and sank into the seat of his chariot, his mind in distress and overwhelmed with grief.' But Lord Krishna explained to him the importance of Karma Yoga and told him the battle of Mahabharata was a battle of Dharma, good overcoming evil. It was a battle of righteousness not for himself but for his countrymen and soldiers. The enemy had to be restrained and/or destroyed. It was Sattva Guna within his soul that enabled him to fulfil his life's purpose of service as a warrior.

Lord Krishna tells Arjun, Bhagavad Gita 2:15-18, 'O Arjun, noblest amongst men, who is not affected by happiness or distress but remains steady in both is eligible for liberation, only the material body is perishable; the embodied soul within is indestructible, immeasurable, and eternal. Therefore, fight O descendent of Bharat.'

In 18:73 Arjun says to Lord Krishna, 'O Achyuta (The Changeless One) my delusion is destroyed, and my memory has been re-gained by me through Your Grace. I am firmly situated; my doubts are gone. I will now act according to your word.'

In the battle of Mahabharata Arjun realizes the Truth and allows his Soul to guide him from within and the Pandavas won the war, which for Arjun was a cleansing of all karma.

The Cherokee tribe of Native Americans have a story about the nature of life that a grandfather tells his grandson, 'It is a terrible fight, and it is between two wolves. One is good. He is beautiful, he is happiness, he is joyful, he is a kind-hearted father, he is a good husband, he is a leader in his community. The other wolf is evil, he is pain, he is suffering, he feels guilt, he feels shame, he feels alone, he feels hopeless and insignificant. The same fight is going on inside you and every other person too.'

When the grandson asks his grandfather which wolf will win the grandfather said, "the one you feed."

Whilst I was studying at a Buddhist monastery in Darjeeling, India I witnessed the blessing of a new baby in the temple. The monk who performed the ceremony brought out an old book that had its pages tied together with a long string and using it as his reference told the mother why her child had chosen them as parents, and what role they would play in helping their child fulfill her karmic duty of service.

But even with this knowledge it does not mean the parents, or the child, will do what is spiritually required of them. In each lifetime we all have been given free will to choose our own path, it is called the grace of God; ultimately only we are accountable for the choices we make as adults.

In my own life and amongst my family I have watched karmic experiences play out again and again. My father, whom I loved dearly, was an addicted gambler. As soon as he got his wages, in those days it was cash, he would go to the club and play cards till it was all gone; I do not recall the winnings. My mother worked hard as a nurse in a busy hospital 7 days a week with one day off a month, but he managed to get her money and gambled with that money too. I remember her hiding some money in the Bible once and praying to God to look after it, but he found that money and gambled and lost it too.

When my dad was 81 years old, he was diagnosed with mesothelioma, a cancer of the lungs that he had got while scraping the asbestos sheets in the factory where he worked. The company he had worked for gave him compensation of a large sum of money. Before he died, he told my mum he was so sorry for gambling all that money and he hoped that the compensation money would have given her some of it back. He felt truly remorseful. I believe his karmic debt was paid in this lifetime.

Pay back always comes back.

An Uncle of mine was guilty of domestic abuse. I remember one time whilst I was visiting their house, I saw him beating his wife so severely, I had never seen anything like that, and it disturbed me for a long time. I knew that that was not the first time he had beaten her so violently.

In her eighties his wife went to live in aged care and my uncle lived on his own. One day some young men broke into his home to steal and beat him violently because he would not give them his credit card, because he did not have one, but they did not believe him. He was found by neighbours and taken to hospital. He survived his injuries but never walked again.

One day whilst I was visiting him in the nursing-home he said to me, "As you sow, so shall you reap." I knew he was referring to karmic retribution in his own life.

When we grasp that awareness of doing wrong that is when we can make it right.

Best-selling author, Louise Hay said, "You have to see the dirt on the plate before you can wash it."

You cannot heal what is not revealed.

Emeritus Professor Thea Brown, co-director of the Deakin Filicide Research Hub at Monash University says that drawing more attention to domestic violence and other forms of abuse is the only way of overcoming it. But she said the problem was so confronting it was a taboo topic.

Those memories created by our feelings, that are saved in the samskara, affect us the most during all our lifetime experiences. They are different from our emotions in that the emotions are an instinctive re-action to an experience, whilst our feelings are an active intelligent faculty of choice that require us to use all our senses. Our feelings constantly change according to the experience. Sometimes our decision is made by an irrational thought that stems from an emotional re-action; but our feelings go deeper and connect deeper to our higher self. The more powerful the feelings at the time of the experience, the stronger the memory that is stored in the samskara.

In a school in the State of Virginia U.S. a six-year-old boy took a gun to school and shot and wounded his teacher. His records showed that he had also choked another teacher until she could hardly breathe, and that on another occasion he had taken off his belt and chased other students trying to whip them. Where was this severe aggressive behaviour coming from? Could it have come from a past memory in his samskara because there were no records of his parents being abusive, or anyone else subjecting him to that kind of treatment.

Young children love playing dressing- up and pretending to be different characters other than themselves, they can even change their voice and make it sound quite different to take on the role they are playing. The more authentic they are in their performance, the more they are immersed in a past life experience, because that strong memory has seeped into their conscious mind.

A teacher told me of a little 5-year-old girl in her class who always became a mum during dress-up time, she would put on her apron, tie a scarf around her head and she would choose the same 5 dolls to be her children, and they always had the same names, she remembered each of them from the oldest to the youngest, Robbie was the middle child.

One day when the teacher was having trouble getting a little boy to do something the girl said, "Miss when I was a mum, and my Robbie wouldn't listen to me I sent him to bed with no supper."

Interestingly she came from a family of two children, the teacher had never seen any of her family members wear scarves around their head, and they never had 'supper' in their own home. The chances of this being a past-life memory are highly likely.

Elaina Smith a 7-year-old from Coventry, in the West Midlands U.K. is a speaker on Mercia's FM radio station. Adult listeners to Mercia's program ask questions related to their personal problems. Elaina listens to their problems and gives them amazingly helpful advice that one would expect from a highly qualified psychologist. When asked where her answers came from Elaina said, "I say whatever comes into my head." Her mother confirmed this when she said, "the advice just comes off the top of her head."

This is another example of a child drawing information from a past life memory that is stored in the samskara as energy in the auric field.

Matias De Stefano is a popular speaker today on past lives as he can recall many previous lives that he has lived here on Earth. One of his most vivid memories of a past life was when he was in Year 3 at school in a history class and the teacher handed him a black and white piece of paper, worksheet, of a pyramid. Instantly he had a strong image of himself as a woman with her husband by her side looking at a huge lion sphinx beside a white pyramid with red temples nearby. The scene included plants and flowers that he/she was in, but the most baffling occurrence was he understood the ancient Atlantean language and not a word of Spanish, his spoken language at the time. He was so confused, sitting there in that history class taking notes in an unknown foreign language with no memory of Spanish!

One of the teachers understood what had happened to him - that he was re-living a past life experience, and knew his Spanish language would return when he was back in his current life, which did happen a couple of hours later, but his mother still took him to a psychologist who diagnosed him as being schizophrenic; years later that same psychologist apologized to him about making such a wrong diagnosis and said Matias had actually helped her to help others by knowing children can slip into a past life if a certain memory is triggered of that past life, like Matias' was in that history class on Egypt.

Today computer scientists and artificial intelligence researchers, A.I. are telling us that memory and intelligence are closely connected. The Hopfield network can, after an initial trigger (associative memory) transport us back in time and a place, when all our brain cells collectively 'fish out' that memory.

A prodigy is a child who has amazing abilities at an early age without being trained to do so. Swami Umeshranand called these prodigies advanced beings who could access the memories of their past lives from their samskara.

David Howell from the U.K. played his first game of chess at the age of five on a second-hand chess set his father had bought at a jumble sale and beat his father. At the age of eight he defeated Grandmaster John Nunn and became the youngest player in the world to defeat a Grandmaster. He became a Grandmaster himself at the age of sixteen, the youngest Briton to ever receive this title.

Serena and Venus Williams, two of the greatest tennis players in the world, started playing tennis from the age of four and were trained by their father Richard Williams who had no coaching experience. He even put together a 78-page plan for their tennis careers.

Henry Ford said, 'Genius is experience. Some seem to think that it is a gift or talent, but it is the fruit of long experiences in many lives.'

Vangelis Papathanassiou the Greek composer said "Orchestration, composition, they teach these things in music schools, but there are some things you can never teach."

He wrote the award-winning music for the movie Chariots of Fire and said he started playing the piano when he was four years old even though he had no formal training and never learned to read notes.

Most people refer to this ability to write stories or music at an advanced level at a young age as a good imagination, but often their knowledge comes from real past life experiences.

Joan Grant shot to fame in London in 1937 when her book 'Winged Pharoah' was published. It was a story of Sekeeta, Pharoah's daughter who lived in pre-dynastic Egypt. In the story Sekeeta had to undergo seven ordeals while shut away in a tomb for four days and nights. Sekeeta passed the test. Joan said the story was a true story that came to her from her 'far memory' because when she wrote it, she had no knowledge of pre-dynastic Egypt. She and her psychiatrist husband Dr. Denys Kelsey left London for France where they set up their 'far memory' therapy sessions and one day a soldier came to see her about his foot that would not stop bleeding, he had been to several doctors, but no sooner did they control the bleeding, it would start up again. Joan 'saw' this soldier in a past-life as a Catholic priest praying fervently to God to receive the holy stigmata – the bleeding hands and feet of Jesus as a sign that he had attained mystical union with Jesus' suffering. Joan relayed this past-life memory to the soldier and told him to acknowledge his worthiness in this life, and the bleeding stopped.

When Joan was 16 years old, she met the writer H.G. Wells and she told him of her 'far memory' stories and he told her she should become a writer when she was older and was, "strong enough to bear being laughed at by fools."

The writer of the Star Wars movies had millions enthralled by his stories of adventure in space, now NASA telescopes have spotted a galaxy far, far away that is the exact image of a TIE Fighter from George Lucas' Star Wars. This galaxy lies in the constellation of Cassiopeia and looks like the spacecraft flown by Darth Vader in Star Wars.

Is it a good imagination or astral travel from a past life experience?

Hannah Bell in her book 'Story men' writes about the Dreaming stories of traditional lawmen of the Ngarinyin people being uncannily like those of Australian author Tim Winton. She said that Tim had been writing stories from a young age that showed a remarkable understanding of the spiritual and cultural rites of the Ngarinyin people when, in fact he had had no contact or background knowledge of them. Where did this deep wisdom come from? Could it be from a past life in an Aboriginal tribe?

Carl Jung said that everyone carried within him or her an eighty-thousand-year-old being. He called it the Ancestral Memory and said, "there is no question that we have access to it."

We think our knowledge is limited but it is unlimited, and that is why people say anything is possible.

In India, a three-year-old, whose parents are illiterate, created his first computer animation program of dancing alphabets. When he turned eight, he began teaching adults computer skills and wrote software programs.

Albert Einstein, at 17, wrote a letter to his friend Zangger in which he said, "I like to occupy my mind with mathematical and physical theorems, that have long been known to me."

The day before my niece was to turn 40, she said to her 7-year-old son Blake, "Today is the last day of me being in my thirties," and he said, "You will be 39 again, when you come back." She asked him what he meant by that? He said, "You won't understand mum."

We all have this ability to access knowledge and wisdom from our past life experiences, and we do, but do not accept they come from what we have learnt or experienced in another lifetime, we try to explain it by saying we must have read it or heard it from somewhere in this life. Those light bulb moments, when the answer or solution pops into our head, is from a past life memory.

Swami Umeshranand told me that people who displayed multiple personalities at one time in this life were acting out memories from the samskara, with many past life identities rolled into this life's personality that makes them display all of them together in this lifetime. This 'bleed through' of their multiple personalities from 3 or 4 past lives overwhelms their conscious mind and disrupts their current life.

There are Sharman's in India who can untangle this overlapping of past life personalities and cleanse the mind to a higher level of purity so that the personality they choose for this lifetime can shine through. The other past life personalities can never be deleted, they are merely subdued.

Rumi, the world's most popular poet said, 'The wound is where the light enters.'

The evolution of all humanity will occur when we accept multiple lifetimes as a truth.

Today more and more people are being healed from physical, mental, and emotional problems through past-life regression therapy. One of the leading professionals in this field is Dr. Brian Weiss. I had the opportunity to attend two of his workshops and witnessed a young man being healed from severe headaches during a past life regression session.

Dr. Weiss took him into a past life experience through deep meditation and hypnosis where the young man was able to recall a past life memory of being chased by a group of men who caught him and knocked him to the ground and started kicking him in the head. His injuries were so severe he died at the scene of the crime.

He was visibly shaken when he came out of that trance-like experience.

Three days after the workshop he told everyone that it had been the longest time in his current life that he had gone without a headache. The young man was carrying such a powerful memory of that past life attack on him that it was affecting him in this lifetime.

In his book, 'Through time into healing,' Dr. Weiss writes about a woman who had reoccurring throat problems that caused her to often lose her voice and have choking episodes. She had seen doctors and ENT specialists but nothing she tried seemed to help. After a past-life regression session with Dr. Weiss she experienced a past life during the Italian Renaissance in which she had been stabbed in the throat. After the regression session her choking attacks disappeared.

Edgar Cayce, pronounced Kay-Cee, had the most past life regression cases documented in the 20th century, more than 14,000! He was born on a farm in Hopkinsville, Kentucky in 1877 and his psychic abilities appeared from early childhood with his 'imaginary friends' whom he said were spirits on the other side. From young he could go into very deep meditation where he said his mind went beyond space and time into the super-conscious mind. He said he only did regression therapy when, "someone's present fate and present suffering remained incomprehensible within the framework of their present life." One case was a young man who came to him with a large red bump between his eyes, that he could neither hide nor explain. Cayce took him into a past life where he was a trader in precious stones in Israel. A fellow trader, who he thought was his friend, hit him on his head, robbed him, and left him to die from a wound to his head when it hit the ground. After this past- life- regression experience the red bump completely disappeared.

Professor Peter Haetsch from Sydney had a man in his thirties go to him for the amputation of his perfectly functioning healthy arm. Professor

Haetsch said, "He was referred to me with a psychiatric letter and he is a perfectly normal guy, he has had a plaster cast on his left arm, and he has had it hidden from his view since his early teens. He has been to see numerous psychiatrists and he wants the limb removed and he hasn't found anyone prepared to do it."

Body Integrity Identity Disorder was first identified in the 18th Century, when a French surgeon was held at gunpoint by a man who demanded his perfectly good leg be removed. Are these memories from past lives?

Likewise, 'Foreign Accent Syndrome' could also be linked to past lives.

Recently on one of those Current Affairs programs on T.V. there was a Chinese woman who after having her tonsils removed woke up speaking with a very strong Irish accent, even though she knew no Irish people, nor had she ever been to Ireland.

And on our news program there was the story of a 19-year-old man who was walking in a park when he suddenly grabbed a young woman by the throat, a stranger; fortunately, another person in the park rushed to her aid and rescued her from the man. Her rescuer said the young man spoke with a strong Russian accent and said he was a 63-year-old Russian woman who needed to kill the girl, who was on the run! When the young man was sentenced to jail, he told the judge he had never been to Russia, couldn't speak the language, nor did he know anyone from that country.

Jack Allan, a former Commonwealth Games swimmer, developed a French accent after suffering a stroke whilst training. He said, "I've spent a lot of time trying to get my British accent back. My goal is to have the French one not leak out at all." Leading doctors diagnosed him with foreign accent syndrome and said it was - 'a rare condition usually triggered by stroke or head trauma.'

I believe these stories of Foreign Accent Syndrome are links to past lives that were triggered when the mind was in an altered state of consciousness, because the language we spoke in a past life is impressed upon the samskara and can manifest in another lifetime.

Our memories of feeling intense fear or pain during our life experiences are our strongest memories in the samskara. Our negative experiences are embedded so deeply in the samskara the possibility of us manifesting them again and again are highly probable.

This is the case in collective karma too when actions committed by a group of people, or one strong personality, can cause other people to have good or bad experiences. The Christian Bible refers to these experiences as the sins of the fathers handed down to seven generations.

The world war that Hitler created and the enormous suffering that came to millions of Jewish people is an example of collective karma because even people who did not want to hurt others were compelled to do so out of fear. This fear caused them to kill and injure others thereby inflicting negative karma in their own samskara that will have to be cleared in another lifetime so they can attain enlightenment.

Rabbi Yonassan Gershom, a Hasidic Jew living near Minneapolis, U.S. had encountered hundreds of people who, he claimed, had died in the Holocaust, and been born again into this present time. One of his case studies was a young Norwegian woman who went to see him because she had suffered nightmares, from a young child, of being in a concentration camp and 'seeing' enormous suffering amongst the people who were prisoners in the camp. There had been no talk or literature around her home of the Holocaust, nor was there any connection between her family and Jewish families, yet she had these persistent nightmares. As the young woman was talking Rabbi Gershom 'saw' another face, thin and emaciated, superimposed on the beautiful young face before him. Softly he started to sing 'Ani Maamin' the hymn sung by many thousands of Jews as they entered the gas chamber. The girl's eyes grew wide with horror, and she broke down in uncontrollable sobs. They both knew that in her past life she had been in a concentration camp. Some weeks later she met up with Rabbi Gershom and she told him the nightmares had stopped and thanked him for helping her to disassociate the old past life traumas that had been draining energy from her current life.

The Delphic Oracle says, "That which wounds also heals."

For that young Norwegian woman, the song 'Ani Maamin' brought back a vivid memory from the past. Today researchers have published, in the Music and Science journal, their discovery that songs bring vivid memories flooding back in what is known as a 'reminiscence bump,' the emotional side of the brain, after therapists used music to successfully help patients with amnesia remember things from their past.

In the 17th century a medical student coined the word nostalgia to describe the anxieties displayed by Swiss mercenaries fighting away from home. Music is a strong trigger of nostalgia. In the Norwegian woman's case the song, Ani Maamin, brought back a memory from her past life that enabled her to release the nightmares she was experiencing in this lifetime.

There is a strong possibility that some of the Jewish people today are the ones who in a past lifetime took the Jewish people to the gas chambers, so that bad karma is with them until they make amends in this life. Their strong voice of condemnation at the Holocaust could be the voices of the perpetrators trying to make amends in this lifetime for the evil they had done in that other lifetime.

I had an experience of this type of reversal of roles when I was teaching at a school in one of the suburbs of Perth where I had dealings with an Aboriginal Elder. One time whilst I was speaking to him a 'white' face kept looking back at me. Behind him was a clear image of a white man from another time.

Many years later this Aboriginal man was jailed for abusing Aboriginal children, and several other crimes. I believe he was a 'white' pioneer from early settlement times who abused Aboriginal people, and then in this lifetime he returned as an Aboriginal man to continue that abuse.

These abusive tendencies and experiences do not stop in one lifetime when they come from the collective karmic pool. In past life regression accounts Swami Umeshranand 'saw' many, many people who had returned to do evil, which he said could only be stopped by doing Japa, sacred rituals. I will share one ritual at the end of this book.

The white men who kidnapped the inhabitants of Africa and shipped them off to America to work as slaves would have a strong possibility of being black men today in America causing misery still to the black population, just in a different colour.

In the Confucian scripture Shu King writes, 'The goal of punishment is to annul the need for punishment through the awakening of the right consciousness.'

Collective karma can only be healed and purified when we serve each other using our light from within.

The Master Jesus was crucified to heal collective karma. Mahatma Gandhi, Martin Luther King, Mother Teresa were all advanced souls who came to Earth to heal the wrongs created by collective karma.

The Hindu God Vishnu said, 'Whenever righteousness wanes and unrighteousness increases, I send myself forth for the protection of good and for the destruction of evil and for the establishment of righteousness. I come into being age after age.' Bhagavad Gita 4:7-8

'Whatever joy there is in this world,
All comes from desiring others to be happy,
And whatever suffering there is in this world,
All comes from desiring myself to be happy.' (Shanti-deva)

Instead of having banners saying, 'Black Lives Matter' we need banners saying, 'All Lives Matter.'

And while we are on that path let us also create a world flag and call it Flag Planet Earth, after all this planet is home to all of us and let us stop calling places third world countries, there is only one world, EARTH, and we all live on it. The only way to establish peace on earth is when we accept the Truth that we are all one big global family. Race, class, gender, religion, material wealth, or lack of it, does not divide us into separate groups of human beings because our spiritual connection has joined us together over many lifetimes here on Earth. There is a beautiful Christian hymn with the words, 'Bind us together Lord, bind us together Lord with cords that cannot be broken. Bind us together Lord, bind us together Lord, bind us together with love,'

Do this simple visualization – Imagine a tiny sun in the middle of your heart that expands with each breath. Feel its heat and power. Now feel this sun in your heart reaching out to the whole Earth – in your imagination go around the globe blessing and healing each country, and all its people, and chant, 'Hai Ma Durga, Hai Ma Durga, Hai Ma Durga, Jai, Jai, Jai Ma.'

The Hindu Goddess Durga (pronounced Du-r-ga) cleanses and heals mother earth. With her many arms she reaches out to all the corners of the Earth and all its peoples, removing poverty, famine, and suffering. Her festival is celebrated during harvest time.

In Korvi Mata, Gujarat, India, and in Darwin, Australia, and many other countries around the world, Christian people come together to pray to the Black Madonna with many stories attesting to her powers to answer their prayers. In the Old Testament Bible, Song of Solomon 1:5 these words – 'I am black; I am beautiful' is our assurance that we are all one, the body colour we choose for our Soul to inhabit during each lifetime does not make us lesser or greater than any other person on Earth.

Our consciousness needs to evolve beyond colour, race, or social standing and this can be achieved when we embrace the truth of re-incarnation. As the Master Jesus said, New Testament Bible, John 18:37 – "For this I was born, and for this I came into the world, to testify to the truth. Everyone who belongs to the truth listens to my voice."

For as long as people continue to deny this fundamental truth, reincarnation, that connects all of life, we will continue to live in darkness, with eyes that do not want to see, and ears that do not want to hear the truth. Unity can only come from a belief system that embraces what is true and discards what is false.

Re-incarnation, when accepted as a truth, can heal this world by giving everyone a clearer understanding of our connection to each other. The belief that we will be back here again and again will emphasize the need to protect this planet, will deepen our connection to others, after all they could have been our family in a past life, like Ken and myself who walked this land together many, many years ago. When I migrated to Australia, I thought I was coming here for the first time. Yes, in this lifetime I was, but I had been here before.

And Ken who was again born in Australia in this life chose to come as a white Australian man, with his connection to Australia going way back. When we were living in a mainly Aboriginal town called Halls Creek my school kids would refer to Ken as, 'he them good white fella, hey Miss?' and they saw me as one of them, "you black fella, like us, hey miss."

Did they feel a deeper connection between us and themselves because of our past life in an Aboriginal tribe? Because in all the time that we lived in Halls Creek we never felt like it was us and them.

We have all lived in different countries during our many lifetimes on Earth. Some people have a feeling of Deja vu when they come to a place for the first time, in their current lifetime. Swiss scholar Arthur Funkhouser gives two examples, Deja visite, already visited, and the second as Deja vecu, already experienced or lived through. As much as 75% of the population say they have experienced some form of déjà vu, and many believe it is related to a past life experience.

French scientist Emile Boirac gave the subject its name in 1876 and said that the experience of déjà vu is usually accompanied by a compelling sense of familiarity, and a sense of eeriness, strangeness, weirdness or what Freud called 'the uncanny' when there is a firm sense that the experience has genuinely happened in the past, even though there is no clear memory of the previous experience. However, that previous experience can be re-called if the memory is in the samskara.

In the Celtic tradition places that feel eerily familiar are called Thin Places. The Celts believe that 'Thin Places' allows us to open ourselves spiritually so we can connect to our true self. They believe that 'Thin Places' awakened our spirit, and allowed the body, mind, and soul to become one so there could be a deeper understanding of the Truth.

Swami Umeshranand believed that a strong feeling towards another country indicated one's connection to that land during a past life.

I did a past life regression on a woman who lived in Australia who felt a strong connection to Germany even though she had never been there, nor did she have any family connections to Germany. The first time she went to Germany, on a holiday with her husband, whilst walking through a forest she felt a strong connection to the area and the feeling of sadness was so intense she cried for days and wanted to return to Perth. For this woman it was a case of déjà vu, because she felt like she had experienced that place before.

During a past life regression session whilst in a deep state of relaxation she witnessed a powerful past life in Germany where she was a four- year-old boy, named Peiter, wearing black shoes with long socks and a beautiful blue and gold outfit, with a flower motif on the top. "It is daytime and warm, and I am going for a walk in the park. I can see my mother at the window of our home, watching me leave. It is a red and white stone building. My mother is upstairs looking out to the park from the window.

My uncle is taking me for a walk. He is a tall man in a long black coat, and he is wearing a black hat, that has a white rim around it. His coat has a religious symbol on it. Me and my uncle are so happy going off on our walk. Alongside the path there is a stream, the water is clear, and I can see the rocks in it. Suddenly I am slipping down the grass, it is happening so fast, my head hits the rocks, I am face down in the water."

Her voice became soft as she continued relating her past life experience to me, "I can see my body, wedged between two rocks, the water is crystal clear.

I am above my body. I am looking at the man's face, my uncle's face, my face is close to his. I am telling him it is not his fault. My mother is looking out of the window, she is looking for me.

I feel sad for my mother. I feel a huge mass of heaviness. My mother needs help, I cannot leave her."

This woman can still access this experience from her samskara, but she does not feel that unexplained sadness anymore, because she understands now that it was connected to a past life experience.

I also had an eerie uncomfortable feeling the first time I visited Singapore, that overcame me each time I visited that country. I felt like I wanted to run away from that place, yet I never knew why.

In September 1964 I boarded the cruise ship P&O Orcades at Bombay, India to come as a migrant to Australia. On our way to Australia, we had two stops, the first was in Penang in Malaysia. We were all very excited to be stopping there for the day and having a look around as tourists. I loved Penang, its balmy weather, and the smell of the food and the happy, smiling faces of the local people was delightful. Australia had an Air Force base there so us speaking English was not a problem. We had the best day there, I also purchased a lovely blouse in Penang that I wore constantly, I liked it so much. Getting back onto the ship everyone was happy and all looking forward to our next port-of-call Singapore. With almost everyone on board ready to disembark as we got into Singapore, I felt excited. The bus took us to Orchard Road and as I stepped off the bus, I began to feel physically ill, was it the bus ride? Was it the humidity? A friend of my parents took us to a nice cool restaurant, but as I sat there, I had this overwhelming feeling 'I don't want to be here!' Fortunately for me an earlier bus was returning to the ship, so my father and I got onto that bus, and I remember feeling so good as soon as I was back on the ship again.

In 1973, I was now married with two sons, my husband got posted to Singapore, so we moved there to live, and I refused to let my first impressions of Singapore cloud the positive aspects of a new job for Ken. But then soon after moving there we had an awful experience.

Our older son, who was five at the time, was walking on the footpath to his friend's house, just two houses down but on the same side as our house, when suddenly we heard loud screams of terror coming from him. Ken and I ran onto the road and saw him being dragged by a man in a car – the car was moving and the male passenger in the car had his door open and was trying to pull our son into their car. They must have heard and seen us because the man let go of our son's arm and the car raced off down the road. Ken picked up our boy, whose legs were covered in blood.

A few months went by and one day whilst our older son was at school and our two-year-old son was in the care of our maid, Ken and I went shopping. When we returned, a couple of hours later I knew something was very wrong, instead of the maid coming to open the gate for us she was nowhere around, and the gate was open! I was out of that car I think before Ken had turned the motor off. Banging on the front door did not bring the maid so I ran around to the back, the back door was open. I was calling out franticly Anita, Anita, Anita – no one answered. I found her in the spare bedroom, gagged and tied to the bed frame. I untied her, Ken was frantically looking for our two-year old son, but he was nowhere to be found. The maid told us three men had broken into the house, gagged her, and tied her up and she didn't know what had happened to our son – and then I found him, locked in a cupboard, curled up in the corner. I got him out, but he wouldn't speak, or cry, he just stared at me, showing no emotion. Ken noticed some red marks around his neck, so we rushed him to the Doctors surgery. The doctor completely checked him over and could not find anything physically wrong with him, so we took him home. I held and carried him a lot, but he would not say a word, from a bubbly, noisy and loud little boy we now had a silent child. I decided to return to Australia so he could be treated by a child therapist. The therapist said he had been completely traumatized, and that fear had stopped him from communicating and not the plastic strap that had been wrapped around his neck by the robbers, to stop him from screaming. I did not let him out of my sight for months, I focused on his throat chakra, took him swimming, and spent time outdoors under the blue sky – this chakra is activated by the colour blue, and then one day he cracked up laughing at his older brother pulling faces and making funny noises, and we had him back again. I returned to Singapore just to pack up my things, and I was so happy to leave that place, vowing to myself I would never go back there again.

The years passed we were living in a beautiful home in the hills just out of Perth, both our boys were doing well at school, I had a good teaching job and Ken had gone over to Singapore to oversee a rig getting fitted out before the rig was put to work in Western Australia. He was to be away for 5 weeks. The boys and I were so busy the five weeks passed quickly, but I was very excited to have him home again, we never liked to be separated from each other for too long. But when he got home, I felt a change in him. He had worked very hard in that humidity in Singapore, I put it down to tiredness, so I was extra patient and loving towards him and completely understood when he said he did not want to go anywhere, even though we had not been out together for over five weeks. And then one day my whole world fell apart; he told me he was leaving me; he had found someone else whom he loved very much, and she was going to have his baby!

This couldn't be true, my head and heart were saying; I adored this man, we had been married for 15 years, he loved me, he loved his sons, what was going on? My head was totally scrambled. Who was she, where did he meet her, what was her name? In Singapore, her name was Jenny. But you can't fall in love with someone in a few days, then the crazy thought came into my head that he fell in love with me just after meeting me, so he can do it?

I went into shock, my whole body started shaking violently – my legs, my arms, even my head. So, was he going to live in Singapore? No, she had just moved over to live in Perth.

I had to get out of there, so I got my car keys and drove off to my mother's house, I just fell into her arms when she opened the door. I had to go back home for my boys and when I got home his car was gone and so were his clothes.

It's funny how the head can switch to automatic because that's what mine did. Then one day I found out where he was staying so I decided to go and visit her at a time I guessed he would be working. I knocked on the door and when this Singaporean woman opened the door, I told her who I was and 'pushed' my way in. It suddenly came to me that she was not pregnant, it was a lie, so I told her that, I also told her Ken would never leave his family so the best thing she could do was return to Singapore. She asked me to leave, and I did. When I got back into my car, I felt good, which I thought was weird.

A few days later Ken was back home, there was no baby, he had put her onto a plane bound for Singapore.

My loathing towards Singapore, a place where I almost lost both my sons, and had, indirectly, almost caused my marriage to break up, continued through the years, though sometimes I did think it might have nothing to do with the place because these experiences could have happened anywhere, as they do, people experience dreadful things all over the world, and I would try hard to let go of the place being the cause of my distress. I had no idea then that it was connected to karma from a past life!

My regression into a past life in Singapore came one afternoon whilst I was in a deep meditative state, and it was so vivid and clear.

'The year was 1888, my name was Clifford Reginald Forbes, I was a Eurasian man living in Singapore, in my early thirties, I was very well dressed, I was fond of wearing a caveat around my neck and my boots were high and were hand made from soft leather and well-polished. I spoke many languages and lived in a grand house with large rooms well furnished with a mixture of exquisite Eastern and English furnishings. The most vivid part of my recollection was the little girl holding my hand. The love I felt for her was so intense it pierced my heart. She was so beautiful, with large soft brown eyes and hair that fell in ringlets down to her waist. She was my pride and joy. She too was well dressed, in a blouse and pinafore dress and her boots too were of the finest leather. I knew I was an extremely wealthy man. Her mother had passed over, but there was no sadness in me, my life felt so complete.'

Then the vision changed.

'I was this old man, bitter and angry with life, sitting in this dingy room that had a bed, a table, and a chair in it. The thought came into my head, 'where is my daughter?' and in a flash she was there, as beautiful as ever but there was a deep sadness in her eyes. She asked me if I needed anything, I said "No." The memory of being duped by a fraudster, a swindler, dominated my mind, how could I have been such an idiot? Conned out of all my money and possessions; how did it happen; why did I let it happen; my daughter tried to warn me, so did others; oh, the unforgivable folly of the mind.' I died in that lifetime having lost all trust in myself and others.

I came out of that trance-like experience clearly being able to see the link between that past life and this lifetime, and Singapore. Upon reflection I saw why there was a negative pattern occurring with Singapore. This is quite common between lives; many people feel drawn to some places in a good way whilst others can feel an instant dislike for certain places.

The traumatic experiences I had in Singapore in this lifetime were connected to that past life when I lived there because I still carried so much negative energy in my samskara from that past life. So, each time I had contact with that country I attracted bad, negative energy into my experiences.

The last memories that I had embedded in my Samskara from that lifetime was total disappointment in myself and others, that was now at a cellular level, like a spiritual illness, in this lifetime. The experiences I had in Singapore in this lifetime was a spiritual course I had to take to heal that memory of despair and bitterness that was still active, at an unconscious level, in my samskara.

Past life regression can break us free from the grip of fate by healing the original wounds and changing negative memories in our samskara, so we can attract the best experiences to ourselves in this lifetime. The lessons I had to learn in this lifetime was Love, Forgiveness, and Trust. In that lifetime I had lost all trust in myself and others. True love is an act of trust; without trust love is not authentic. This includes self-love.

Interestingly I was in Singapore a few years ago when my son and his family went to live there, and I decided to pay them a visit, the house and area they lived in looked familiar, Saunders Street, Emerald Hill, for me it was a sense of Deja-vu, it felt as if I had been there before, even though it was my first visit to that area in this current lifetime. Was it from that past life memory in my samskara? But this time I felt at ease in Singapore.

I was given tough lessons and experiences in Singapore to guide me to my highest good that enabled me to move onto a loving relationship with my husband that was the best outcome for myself, him, and our sons. Holding onto grudges lifetime after lifetime stops us from entering Samadhi, enlightenment. The spiritual advancement that we make in each lifetime will very likely be preceded by emotionally painful experiences.

At Ken's funeral, by far the saddest day of my life in this lifetime, an enormous loneliness engulfed me as I gazed at his coffin, draped in the altar cloth on which lay the beautiful arrangement of native Australian flowers that he loved. Gazing at his face, in his photograph near the flowers, the thought came into my head 'I am a better person because of you.'

Was it my thoughts or was it Ken's? I believe we both had the same thought at the same time. Couples who have spent many years together often think the same thoughts simultaneously, and we had had the same thought, at the same time, there in that church at his funeral. For me it was further proof that death cannot separate us spiritually. Then I was singing the words in a hymn 'endless is the victory thou over death has won.'

Time exists in a unified field of consciousness called the quantum field where all events are occurring via our memory. Our Soul is a quantum-informed model of primordial consciousness. Choices made during our life are about whether we chose to do something, how we do it, what we respond to, and how we respond. Our memories from our past lives determines how we live our present life. If the memories are negative, we attract negative experiences into our current life again and again until those negative past-life memories are dissolved. Once this karmic burden is lifted our life path becomes more beautiful as we evolve to higher levels of consciousness. That is our purpose for coming back again and again, to dissolve all Karma.

Some years ago, I did a past life regression on a woman who went from one past life into another and then into another rapidly. It was as if her unconscious mind wanted to clear everything negative from her memory field in one fell swoop!

In her first regression she was a little boy in that lifetime hiding under stairs. There were many rooms in the cottage, but he was too frightened to go into any of them. The little boy felt very cold under the stairs. He was hiding from his father, who was mean and cruel. My client said, "I don't want to be here." And with that she went into another past life memory of another traumatic experience. In this second lifetime she was a woman working in a store when some men came into the store and one of them raped her. She pleaded with the others to help her, but no one did.

Next, she slipped into a completely different lifetime where she was Carol a woman in Italy. "I am walking along the beach on the sand holding my little girl's hand. Her name is Pia, and she is three years old. I can see her very clearly; she has lovely black hair and green eyes. She has beautiful green eyes. Pia is holding a small wooden horse in her hand. I bought it for her. The man is waiting for her. I tell Pia to go to the man. I am not going any further. She is going to the man. Pia does as she is told."

My client said this last sentence in a very cold, detached voice. Nothing like the voice she was using before, which had been very soft, almost to the point where I could barely hear her. Then complete silence. I asked her what was happening now. And she said, quite loudly "I have my money I am going." We both sat in silence again, and then my client started crying and said she didn't want to talk about it anymore, so I told her I would slowly count to 5 and she could come out of that memory. Then we sat in more silence. My client said she felt enormous sadness, so we did a short meditation together. When she came out of the meditation, she said she felt better and left.

The next day I received a message from her, 'I am feeling like I have been run over by a bus and very emotional, I had a very restless night, and more images came through.'

A few days later her husband bought her a beautiful green, emerald ring which, according to crystal lore, is the gemstone of unconditional love. It made my client think of Pia and her beautiful eyes.

Some days later she came back to see me. I asked her to go into that life with Pia and she was instantly able to re-call what happened after she gave Pia away.

"I took the money and went to the market. I want my little girl back. I must get her back." Silence. I asked her to tell me what was happening. She said 'I cannot find the man. No one has heard of him.' Tears welled up in her eyes and she had difficulty speaking while re-calling that past life. After a brief pause, she said, 'I don't know what to do.' She then saw herself in that lifetime as Carol lying on the floor begging God to bring Pia back to her. She tells God she is very sorry for what she did, she made a mistake. Pia is her child, her baby. Please can she have her back, she is sorry. She will look after Pia for the rest of her life she promises God if He will give Pia back to her. She is looking amongst the boats at the harbour asking people if they have seen her little girl. The police helped her. She waits in a small cell-like room. The police came to her with Pia. She is overwhelmed with tears of joy.'

In that lifetime my client saw an image of Carol and Pia living a happy life together, with the two of them being inseparable. Carol never told anyone how Pia became a missing child, her shame was too great. Only the man who took Pia knew her secret.

In this lifetime my client has experienced a lot of shame and hurt. Her father was an abusive man who physically and sexually abused her mother, some of it she witnessed at a very young age. As a teenager she herself was sexually abused by a man and her first husband physically beat her, even in front of one of their friends and when she asked the friend to help her, he just walked away, because he didn't want to get involved.

Today my client's life is one of abundance in ways she could never have imagined. Her second husband is her soul mate, and she says her blessings never cease to amaze her. She has forgiven her father and can even feel love for him, knowing his years of alcohol abuse caused him to behave in the way he did, and she has let go of feelings of shame. Every day she thanks God for clearing her emotional baggage. Soon after her regression therapy her creative abilities blossomed and she started painting, some of her art works are truly magnificent. Her karma from those past lives have been resolved.

When we consciously address powerful memories from the past, we become more accepting of ourselves and others, and can then turn those painful memories, energies, into creative expressions.

Do this simple heart mudra by pressing your thumbs together facing downwards and bending your fingers and bringing them together to form a heart shape and say, "I lovingly create my own reality." Your left thumb represents Love, and your right thumb represents Trust.

In life we do not play the 'blame' game because it becomes a pattern of deflecting blame on others and blocks healing from happening. Blaming others for what happens in our life comes from the ego, 'I haven't done anything wrong, it's someone else's fault.' Often the ego wants us to stay entangled with the memory of the experience, and how awful the person was to do that to us, until it suffocates us and stops us from moving forward.

The saying, 'Adam blamed Eve, Eve blamed the serpent, and the serpent never had a leg to stand on,' shows the folly of playing the blame game.

The same can be said for complaining; constantly complaining about our lot in life, or others, also stops us from moving forward. I learnt a very valuable exercise when I was at Isha Yoga Centre in Coimbatore, India. Sit in a crossed legged position with your hands on your knees and let your thumbs touch your pointer fingers. Stretch out the other three fingers. Imagine your thumbs and pointer fingers are forming a zero, and with your eyes closed keep saying, 'zero complaining, zero complaining' for as long as you can. This simple exercise will get you out of the habitual pattern of complaining and give you more energy to live your life with a contented and more peaceful mind.

All of us have died in a past life so we can be here in this life, those deaths could have been tragic, or peaceful whilst sleeping. But all those memories are there stored in the samskara's energy field. People who are afraid of dying might have had a bad death experience in another lifetime. Once you embrace the process of death, life, and re-birth, the thought of death holds no fear. As Sri Aurobindo said, 'Life is death, and death is life.'

Our self-development continues across lifetimes as our ability to see the big picture in every situation grows so we can see the good that can come out of the worst situations. This develops humility and gratitude, as our ideas of grandeur and our ego are slowly destroyed.

The great philosopher Socrates was condemned to death for crimes he had never committed. He showed great courage and goodness of heart when he said, "Men of Athens I have the warmest affection for you, but I shall obey God, and while I have life, I will never cease from my practice of teaching philosophy, and to saying to all I meet to seek virtue."

The Master Jesus showed only love to the people who crucified him. Enlightened Souls do not feel hate or malice, they feel blessedness in every situation believing even their suffering can be an awakening for themselves and/or others.

Swami Umeshranand said, "the illumined souls are never one-sided or narrow-minded. Their enlarged vision embraces all, thereby releasing them from the bondage of karma."

My mother always told us to 'Count your blessings,' and, 'get over it,' when we were children and were going on and on over the same issue that usually involved us feeling sorry for ourselves, or 'hard done by'- as she put it.

Good can come out of even the worst situations; if we look for it, we will find it in service to others. In Carol's story her mistake of selling Pia, then getting the Police involved in finding her was an act of service because it might have stopped that man, in that lifetime, from child trafficking.

My husband Ken was given an opportunity to serve shortly before he died. Whilst in hospital, in a ward on his own, where he spent most of his time sleeping because he was so weak, a nurse came into his ward, around 10pm, and got an assistant to wheel him in his bed into a two-bed ward where there was another patient lying in another bed. My husband drifted back to semi sleep but became fully awake when he heard sobs coming from the other man. Ken spent the night comforting this stranger who had attempted suicide and was consumed with despair and a feeling of hopelessness.

Early the next morning I went to visit my husband in hospital, only to find him not in his room. I immediately felt anxious, 'where had they taken him?' A nurse took me to the ward where he was asleep. The young man said to me, "he is pretty worn out, it is my fault, I kept him up all night." Then he went on to say, "I love this man, I was lying in my bed, calling out to God for help, asking him to take my life, and God sent me a friend; I truly love this man and I will never forget him." I asked him why he was in hospital? He said he had had a difficult childhood and now at 23 years he had cancer and did not want to live, he said he saw no reason for living, until he met Ken. Ken had told him his life was important, and that he could do a lot of good in the world once he overcame cancer, he could still live a good life and be happy. The young man told me that after talking all night to Ken he was determined to get well and live a full life and help others, just as Ken had helped him.

A nurse arrived around 8am, with an assistant and Ken was taken back to his original ward, and as they were wheeling Ken out of the two-bed ward the young man said, 'I will never forget you man, I love you man." Ken was moved into that two-bed ward just for that one night, so he could serve. A few days after that we lost Ken to cancer. He had completed his last duty of service. I hope and pray that that young man is getting on with his life, here on earth, serving others.

'Just as the caterpillar thought his world had come to an end it changed into a butterfly.' When we accept re-incarnation as a truth a metamorphosis will occur.

From the Bhagavad Gita 2:22, 'Worn-out garments are shed by the body; worn out bodies are shed by the dweller within the body. New bodies are donned by the dweller, like garments.'

When someone leaves this life via suicide the feelings of despair that overwhelms the mind stays in their samskara and in their next life they access these same feelings of despair each time life becomes difficult, thereby increasing the intensity of their negative thoughts. Today science is telling us that our body is constantly creating new cells and if there is anger, fear, and disappointment, in the emotions (connected to the limbic brain) we make new cells of anger, fear, and disappointment. Therefore, in our current life it is harder for us to escape from these negative feelings, that has now brought about a chemical imbalance in the brain, that is hard to understand and live with. It is like having a bigger dose of everything that is negative because it is enhanced by the memory in the samskara from a past life AND from this life.

Throughout life old patterns, like a written script, may continue to cause suffering because all of them are rooted in the energy body, samskara.

Many past-life regressions have shown that most people choose their parents before they come to earth.

My teacher Swami Umeshranand said that was true, but that some souls were in such a hurry to return to earth, they came to whoever would accept them. In this scenario some souls will evolve to higher states of consciousness, whilst others might regress to lower states of consciousness, depending on their parents' level of consciousness. Parents with high levels of Sattva Guna will help their children to serve with humility, whilst those with high levels of Rajas Guna will influence them to take whatever they can, regardless of how it affects others.

Today many babies are being born through egg and sperm donors. Adam Hooper in Perth, Western Australia, said he has fathered over 26 children but did not know whether he would play a part in their lives as it depended on what the child's legal parents wanted. This means that babies are choosing parents who are not their biological parents.

Betty Eadie in her book, 'Embraced by the Light' wrote about the baby girl that came to her from 'out of the blue.' After having seven children she decided to have a hysterectomy due to health issues. Six years later her sister told her about a young woman who was pregnant, but due to family problems couldn't keep the baby and asked Betty if she could keep the baby for a couple of months until the baby could be placed with adoptive parents.

Betty took the baby home after she was born and there was an instant bond between them. Her husband and their children loved her too and would take her out of her crib to play with her as soon as she woke up. The two months passed but suitable parents were not found for the baby girl and by now Betty said, "I had forgotten that she wasn't mine."

Ten and a half months later the call came – the Adoption Agency had found relatives of the baby to adopt her. Betty said, "We had known all along she couldn't be ours, but now I was in the worst agony a mother can know. I was about to lose my child."

When the new parents drove up, she carried the baby to the car and handed her to her new mother. Betty said, "She realized that she was being taken away from me and began to scream. My heart broke. The vision of my precious little girl crying with hands outstretched, reaching for me, burned into my soul."

For a short while after this Betty went into deep depression, her spirit broken down. Three and a half months later she got a call from the Adoption Agency, it was 'bad news' the baby was in hospital- the adoptive father had been drinking and couldn't take her crying anymore and had thrown her down a flight of stairs. For two weeks she was critically ill in hospital but even though her injuries had been taken care of the doctors feared that in her emotional state the baby might never recover.

Betty phoned her husband Joe at work and told him. He rushed home and took her to the airport to get a flight to where the baby was. When the woman from the Adoption Agency handed the baby to her, Betty said "She recognized me immediately and clutched me tightly with both her arms and little legs wrapped tightly around me. What have they done? What have they done? I cried."

Betty took 'her' baby home and said, "I wrapped her in a dish towel and tied her to my body. She and I spent a few months tied together like this."

She and her husband hired an attorney, and the courts ruled that the child's health depended on the continuous stable life she received from Betty and Joe and allowed them to legally adopt her. They named her Betty Jean.

This true story illustrates the undeniable truth that baby Betty Jean chose her parents, even though her adoptive mother was unable to physically have a child.

Betty had a vision of this child long before she came to be part of their family. After her hysterectomy operation, one day whilst her husband was visiting her in hospital, she saw a little 'spirit girl' in the room – "A golden halo of light emanated from her, glowing in the room wherever she walked. I asked Joe if he could see her. He couldn't. I sensed her inner joy. She then faded from my view and never reappeared, but I knew I would never forget her."

In her book, 'Embraced by the Light' Betty endorses re-incarnation and the belief that children choose their parents when she said, "I knew also that while she could not be born to me because of my hysterectomy she had found another way to become a part of my life. We were closest of friends forever, eternities of experiences behind us, and eternities ahead."

The Master Jesus said, John 10:10; 'I AM come that they might have life, and that they might have it more abundantly.'

A young man named Jeff, not his real name, told me his interesting story of how he was chosen by souls from the other side to be their father in their next life.

When he was in his late teens, he had a vision one day in which he was a gardener cutting and shaping a hedge with a powerful wiper snipper when from the corner of his eye he noticed a boy standing nearby, the boy started to move closer, and then he noticed a little girl behind him. He said to the boy, "You need to move away, this is dangerous, you could get hurt if you come too close." The boy did not move, he just stood there, watching Jeff, and so did the little girl. Jeff said, "Who are you?" And he said, "I am your son." Jeff laughed and said, "I don't have any children, neither am I going to have any, so off you go." The boy left, but the girl came closer.

Jeff looked at her and she said, "I am your daughter Lily!" And she left.

Some years later Jeff and his partner had a son, Jeff was the first one to hold him as he was born, and they had an amazing bond from that moment. Sadly, the relationship between Jeff and his partner did not last and he had a difficult time trying to get to see his son. He spent a long time separated from him and that caused a lot of suffering for both. Finally, he got time to spend with his son and life became happier for them. Years later Jeff got a new woman in his life, she had a son too, from a previous relationship, and neither of them wanted anymore children. The two boys got on well and life was going on nicely when his partner discovered she was pregnant. To put it lightly, Jeff was not happy. Lily arrived and she is the apple of Jeff's eye and much loved by all.

My son also had a strange experience whilst living in Canberra, Australia. One evening whilst in the shower he heard the front doorbell ring, he ignored it at first but when it kept on ringing, he got out of the shower, put on a dressing gown, and went to the front door and opened it. An elderly man stood outside, in the rain, and said to my son, "Is Tom here?" My son said, "No there is no Tom here." The man, still standing in the rain said, "What, no Tom here!" My son said, "No" and the man disappeared! My son stepped out, into the rain, and walked down the pathway but could not see anyone, nor did he hear or see a car. He was completely confused, where had the old man gone and how had he disappeared so fast? Sixteen years later my son had a son and called him Tom, five years later he had another son, Alex. From the moment Alex could move around he wanted to be with Tom. He was so attached to his older brother he wanted to be with him all the time, sometimes even in his bed at night. Could Alex have been the visitor, from the other side, my son had all those years ago enquiring about Tom on that rainy night in Canberra?

Most children are loved and nurtured by their parents but what about the ones who are abused and ill- treated by their parents? If they chose them, why did they? Did they have some harsh karmic lessons to learn so their higher self could break through the bondage, darkness, of a wrong committed in a previous life?

"Through faith women received their dead relatives, raised to life again. Others, refusing to accept freedom died under torture, to be raised to a better life." Bible Hebrews 11:35

SEXUAL ABUSE AND KARMA

Ashley Rinehart told her story to the world of being raped by her father from the age of five, she had no childhood of joy and childlike innocence. When she was 13 her father built a secure dungeon like room under their house and locked her in there so she could be his sex slave. He told anyone who asked after her that she had run away, with, "You know what teenagers are like?" At 13 she had her first child to him, with only the minimum of care that he was able to give her. She had three more children to him, and they all lived in that room, never seeing anyone except this evil man. Years passed until Ashley's two sisters went to the police when they discovered this terrible thing that was going on, in the basement of their home, with their sister. The father is now serving a life sentence in prison; the judge said he showed no remorse. In other words, he showed no feelings for the heinous crimes he had committed.

What will his karmic experiences be in his next life? And what will Ashley's be? Will he come back to make a wrong right? Or will the pattern of abusing a child be so strong in his memory, samskara, that he will repeat that behaviour?

What about Ashley? Were her experiences pay-back for past life wrongs she had committed? If she opens her heart to compassion towards others through service she can heal from all bad karma, memories, and replace them with positive loving memories. Sometimes even the wrong path is part of finding the right path, when we go in pursuit of the Truth.

Jimmy Barnes, a famous Australian singer wrote in his book, Working Class Man, "The truth is the most important thing in the world – sometimes hearing it is harder than telling it. There are a lot of things we can't control in life. Avoidance makes most situations worse because nothing is resolved."

Here then is the key to healing sexual abuse – The Truth which the Master Jesus said would set us free. This is freedom from the pain and shame of sexual abuse becoming part of the unresolved memories in the samskara, that stop us from evolving to higher levels of consciousness.

From the beginning of human life on Earth abusing another sexually has affected the balance, the equilibrium, of the whole community because it continues over lifetimes, via the memory in the Samskara. Gerry Georgatos in his story Survivor said 'my young years were lived in a time in the early 1970s of impenetrable hideous silences. I had nowhere to turn. There was hostility to such truth, whilst also widespread disbelief of such happenings. Forty-seven years later I finally told my partner. The telling was traumatic.'

According to Gerry, 'Trauma that remains unaddressed and unresolved cannot heal and where there's no healing, trauma becomes cumulative, languishing as disordered thinking and negative selves. Unaddressed child sexual abuse is one of the worst forms of trauma which can degenerate to toxic, internalized grief.'

Sexual abuse will continue in our society due to secrecy, silence, and shame. The only way to cleanse this karmic sin is to express it and make the abuser accountable in this current lifetime to stop it from continuing. Sexual abuse suppressed causes the heart to carry a lot of pain through a feeling of unworthiness. This pain remains in the samskara until it is healed. Singer-songwriter Kate Millar-Heidke used her song You Can't Hurt Me Anymore to release the pain and trauma of being sexually abused by her great-grandfather. She said the actions of other sexually abused women gave her the strength to tell her story through her music.

As a child I loved playing hide-n-seek. My parents had gone out one evening and left me and a relative of mine in the care of our ayah, maid, I was about 5 years old, and she was 6. The ayah must have gone to her quarters, way down the back of the property and left the two of us playing together when her teenage son joined us and suggested we play hide-n-seek, and I was IT, so the two of them went off to hide. I looked and looked but because we were playing the game in the dark, with no lights on, I could not find them. Being a child who never wanted to give up I kept going and there they were but instead of squealing because they had been found there was dreadful silence. The boy grabbed my hand and placed it on his very erect penis, that my relative was also holding on to. I said "NO" in my loudest voice and grabbed my relative's hand and we both ran off.

The next morning, being an early riser, I went into my parents' bedroom and casually said, "We played hide-n-seek last night and the chokra made us hold his willy!"

My dad jumped out of the bed with such anger and speed I thought I had done something wrong, and he swore – we knew them as bad words that you never said. But he raced past me and ran off to the servants' quarters at the back and we never saw that teenage boy again.

I had no idea this story was in my memory until my relative reminded me about it, some 60 years later, after she had heard something on the news about child sexual abuse. She said she had been terrified with fear, when he had grabbed her hand and would not let her go. Me coming along and saying NO, broke that feeling of fear that she was in and gave her the courage to run away with me; and then me speaking about it the next morning to my parents stopped, what would have been a soul-destroying experience for both of us, from happening again.

Not so for a family I know that have had sexual abuse in their family for 100 years because no one spoke up.

It started with the mother, Doris, not her real name. Doris lived on a farm in Western Australia and every morning she had to go into her fathers' bed and hold his penis and 'play' with it, sometimes her little sister had to do it too. Years later the sister told me that when she became an adult, she hated that part of a man's body so much that when she gave birth to a son, she had moments when she wanted to cut his penis off – thank God that didn't happen.

Before her 18th birthday, Doris got pregnant to the guy she was friendly with at the time, so they got married, but when she mis-carried that baby he left her saying she never was pregnant, and she had only made up that story to get him to marry her. At that time her younger sister was engaged to the local butcher, but Doris got involved with him and got pregnant and had a baby girl. The baby's father, the butcher, as soon as he found out Doris was pregnant with his child had nothing more to do with either of the sisters. Doris went to work on a sheep farm in Kellerberrin some 180kms from Perth with her little daughter. She cooked the meals for the shearers. One day a shearer raped her near the kitchen, and she got pregnant, when she told the sheep station owner's wife she was raped and was pregnant she told Doris to leave immediately with her small child because she didn't want any trouble. Doris returned to Perth and got a room with a kind woman and stayed with her until her baby boy was born. Some years later she met a man whom she had known as a teenager and she had a son by him, but he too didn't want her or the child. She told me he was the only man she had truly loved. She now had three children and was homeless with no support.

Then one day she met someone who told her that the man she had married was a soldier in the army and was posted in a war zone and if she took her marriage certificate to the army offices she could receive a pension, which she did, and to her great relief she was given a pension, even though he had enlisted into the army as a single man. Later, through the army she was able to purchase some land to farm. After the war her husband, whom she had not seen for years, returned to Perth, and joined her on the farm. Years later her husband sexually abused her daughter and made her pregnant, but the baby was aborted. It was a family secret, so it festered on – Doris' father was an abuser, so was her husband, and so was her son, and her grandson, because her great- grandchild and two grandchildren suffered from the same fate.

Silence, through a feeling of fear and shame, protects the perpetrators and this is karmically doing them more harm, along with the victims, because their souls are unable to be completely free and open to the joys of life, the victim and abuser stay in a place of bondage in this lifetime and tragically they return to their next life with that hideous memory in their samskara, because a family pattern of sexual abuse has been established that cannot be removed until it is healed because, you cannot heal what is not revealed. The abuse must be exposed and dealt with as a serious wrong, never to be repeated; not swept under the carpet, hoping it will go away. It can't go away – it is part of the memory field, so a stronger memory of punishment and acknowledging its wrongness must be created in the samskara, or karmic retribution will happen, in one form or another. Not reporting it and dealing with it appropriately allows it to fester, so it gets played out again and again in other lifetimes, over many generations, because it now has become generational abuse, that can last up to the seventh generation, according to Biblical law.

Had Doris spoken truthfully about her own sexual abuse and the damage that that abuse had done to her and her sister, her whole family would have seen it as a wrong never to be repeated. Instead, her silence, and the silence of others allowed it to fester like an insidious disease. Sharman's call this prolonged form of suffering the 'collective nightmare' because intergenerational trauma gets passed through our family lineage.

This silence also played out in her sister's family. One of her daughters was abused by their brother, and the other daughter married a man who sexually abused their daughter. Getting to the truth of the matter and never being afraid of the truth must be instilled in children from young.

Today massive steps are being taken to eliminate sexual abuse from almost every country on Earth. In some places in India people are seeking capital punishment for those who rape children. Human beings are being guided to move into a higher state of consciousness. Wanting to feel good is synonymous with wanting to feel God, our higher self, because God IS good and all that the Divine creator created is good. As we open up to this Divine power, that we all carry within us, more people will have the strength and courage to speak out against sexual abuse, and this inner strength will bring healing to themselves and others, like Grace Tame, 2021 Australian of the Year, a woman who survived sexual abuse and made it her mission to fight for others, who said, "I spent almost my entire life feeling disgusted, ashamed and in denial about what happened to me and, what I had allowed myself to do and be a part of. Then one day, I stopped. I stopped running away and I looked at myself. I looked into the pain and what I saw was that I was ready to leave it all behind and heal."

This is karmic cleansing, and everyone can do it when they draw on their strength from within. It is simple human nature to want to highlight the good and conceal the bad. Bridget Malcolm said via social media that her disturbing dreams and nightmares stopped soon after she had the courage to report the sexual abuse that she suffered at the hands of her music teacher in her early teens.

Swami Vivekananda said, "Arise, Awake! Awake from this hypnotism of weakness, none is weak; the soul is infinite, omnipotent, and omniscient. Stand up, assert yourself, proclaim the God within you, call upon the sleeping soul and see how it awakes. Power will come, goodness will come, purity will come when this sleeping soul is roused to Self-conscious activity."

With the support of wonderful people around, professionals, and others, victims of sexual abuse will discover that they do not need to protect perpetrators of sexual violence through the power of shame. They can step into freedom. From the darkness they can move into the light.

Here is a healing visualization to heal the trauma of sexual abuse.

First you need to imagine light – not from electricity, or candles, or sunlight, or moonlight. Just see light by telling yourself, "I see light all around me." Practice this a few times until you get good at imagining spiritual light.

Then do this visualization:

You are standing in a room full of LIGHT.

Feel this light as energy all around you.

Just stand in this light.

Keep absorbing this light into every cell in your body.

It radiates out of your body into your energy field around you.

You and the Light are one.

Feel and see a Being of light approach you.

A golden medal hanging from a gold ribbon is placed by the Being of light around your neck.

Hold the medal in your hand near your heart.

Lift the medal and look at it.

See the word Truth engraved on it.

Let a feeling of blessedness flow through you.

When you are ready come out of this visualization, and if you want to make it more powerful find a medal and have the word TRUTH engraved on it.

I know someone who had the word truth tattooed on her arm, and it changed her life for the better.

This visualization also forgives any blame towards yourself.

Forgiveness is about empowering yourself, rather than empowering your past.

The Angels sing with halleluiahs whenever we overcome our demons. Living a life of denial, even unable to admit to oneself our mistakes of the past, increases one's bad karma because it alters our behaviour, we are all beautiful souls within, something you have done does not have to constitute the sum of who you are. We are all human and we have all made mistakes.

Victims of sexual abuse often turn to alcohol or drugs or violence, or homelessness because they cannot cope with the abuse and the inner turmoil of that abuse.

I know a woman who has a truly compassionate heart, yet she would put her kind, gentle husband through the worst verbal abuse over the smallest of issues, then further punish him by leaving him, destroying his personal items and so on. Then she would come back, only to make him suffer emotionally, physically, and mentally again and again. When I heard her story, I was overcome with sadness. From about the age of ten her father would come home with two or three 'mates' yelling at her to cook them tea (dinner) and after they had eaten each would sexually abuse her, then leave, whilst she cried herself to sleep. Sometimes her father even made her clean up the mess they had made in the kitchen. Later in life this hurt and confused woman left her home country and made a new life for herself marrying a kind, quiet man who worked hard to give her all the comforts in life, including his love, that she repaid with meanness.

Here is an example of more bad karma being manifested for her. Her demons from the past were blocking her from doing good by making her hurt her innocent husband while she kept the pain and shame to herself, and those men who abused her were not punished or made accountable for their evil acts in any way whatsoever.

According to Swami Umeshranand this creates karmic enmeshment with the possibility of them all coming together in another lifetime to continue the abuse. For the victims this is a horrible thought, 'I will be with those molesters, monsters, again!' But until they expose these people and make a wrong right, with the power of truth, the samskara is not cleansed from the pain and shame of those experiences, their silence out of fear creates the darkness, this denies the Light from shining in their samskara.

Only by bringing it to the light and releasing the fear can they break the cord of karmic enmeshment. Ted Andrews in his book, How to Uncover Your Past Lives says, 'The child is born into a home according to parental perceptions, heredity, environment, past life and karmic ties.'

The pain and suffering we cause to another cause's negative karma in the samskara, and until this back log is cleared, we will be drawing negative experiences to ourselves. Our denial of the truth through silence indirectly protects the abusers and this creates bad karma for the victim, because evil ignored is evil repeated, and indirectly they are the cause of another, or more people/children being abused. Silence validates the abuser to believe they have done nothing wrong, but if the victim uses their experience as an opportunity to do good, they will inspire others to speak their truth. By speaking out you protect others, then only can you 'walk your talk' when you walk your path of TRUTH. By bringing the abuse into the open the victim is surrendering it to the light, they have let go of fear, which is darkness, by allowing the light to cut through all the barriers towards healing these experiences from their samskara. This is the aim in every lifetime, to destroy the darkness and let in the light and become enlightened. Healing does not come through denial but through surrendering to our highest Self, our Godliness. For victims of abuse moving forward is difficult because they must change to new ways of thinking and feeling.

It is like the story of the farmer who tried to move his cows from a very dry pasture to a lusher pasture on the other side of his farm. Before letting them wander freely in the lush new pasture he moved them into a holding pen. Some cows stayed near the gate wanting to go back to the dried-up land, the place they knew and were familiar with. Other cows moved on through the cattle chutes, where health checks were made, a bit confining but soon they were moved into beautiful green pastures. They were the lucky ones, they detached themselves from the old barren pasture and welcomed the lush new pastures and were perfectly content. While the others still clung to the gates and would not enter the cow chutes. They could not let go of the old place, as barren as it was, through fear. Sometimes we must go through a complicated process to enter the fields of greener pastures.

In the Old Testament Bible, in the book of Daniel, there is the story of Daniel who showed no fear in what can only be described as the most terrifying experience anyone could ever experience.

Daniel was an Israelite who had been captured by the Babylonians in 650 A.D. He worked for King Darius as one of his political officials. Over time Daniel and the King became more and more like good friends with the King often seeking out his company. This made the other officials jealous and annoyed; they were Babylonians and Daniel was not, and to make the situation worse Daniel prayed to a God they could not understand. So, they plotted to get him removed from the King's service. They petitioned the King to make a law whereby people could pray only to King Darius, and honour only him; then, they set out to trap Daniel. They watched his every move and when they saw and heard him praying to his God, they arrested him for breaking King Darius rule – as King and Sovereign everyone prayed only to him. When Daniel was brought before King Darius the King was devastated, not for a moment did he think that rule applied even to his friend Daniel. At that time there was only one punishment for offenders, Daniel was thrown into a pit full of hungry lions. That night the King never ate or slept; his heart felt broken. Early the next morning he went to the pit and to his utter amazement Daniel was alive, and so were all the lions! The King had Daniel taken out of the pit and he asked him how had he survived? Daniel told him he had prayed continuously to God; his faith and trust were so strong he felt no fear, and that made the lions stay away from him.

Say this affirmation:

Let me rise above all doubt and fear.

Let my intention be strong and clear.

No matter what appears to be.

I stay anchored in my Divinity.

Our Divinity is with the Truth that the Master Jesus said would set us free.

This is freedom from the continuous cycle of death, birth, death, re-birth, that goes on and on until our Divinity is one with God.

In The Buddhist Doctrine of Karma and re-birth by Narada Maha Thera, he states that when Buddha received enlightenment, he had visions of all his past lives and when he gave his followers the Four Noble Truths, he concluded with the words, "Ayam antima jati natthi dani punabbhao" meaning, "This is my last birth. Now there is no more re-birth." Amyutta Nikaya verse 420

Do this visualization called 'The Big Bubble' and it will give you the power to always speak your truth, to understand the truth, to intuitively know the truth, and to draw people to you who honour the truth.

Quieten your mind by softly and deeply breathing and silently saying calm, calm, calm. Imagine you are in a large transparent rainbow coloured bubble. Now feel TRUTH everywhere in the air- space in the bubble. As you breathe in feel the breath filling your head and heart, and then moving out slowly from your hands as you exhale, allowing the untruths to escape through the palms of your hands. Breathe in deeply again and allow the breath to follow through your head and heart, and as you breathe out, let all the lies and untruths from this life and past lives flow out of your hands, into the translucent rainbow bubble.

Do this for as long as you can, staying in the rainbow bubble to help you live your life of truth by emanating the truth from within you, whilst also drawing it from others, back to you. Our purpose for coming to Earth is to serve. Your story can be life changing for another because it allows their body, mind, and soul, to find and feel the peace after their traumatic experiences. Swami Umeshranand called this place of realization, 'inner serenity.'

This is another good affirmation to say often.

In the infinity of life where I Am all is perfect, whole, and complete.

I Am always Divinely protected and guided.

I now choose to rise above my problems and recognize the magnificence of my being.

All is well in my world.

There is an old Greek fable called North Wind and the Sun. 'North Wind and Sun were arguing as to who was more powerful. Each felt their power was greater than the other. So, to prove who was more powerful they decided to test their skills on a shepherd boy, who was walking down a pathway with his cloak on, as to which one out of the two of them could get the shepherd boy to take his cloak off?

North Wind said, "I can get the boy to remove his cloak" so he blew and blew, but the shepherd boys' cloak would not blow off, it just made the boy hang onto it with both hands even tighter. The Wind was so strong it nearly blew the shepherd boy over, but still he clung onto his cloak. After the allocated time North Wind reluctantly gave up.

Now it was the Sun's turn. The Sun made its light brighter and stronger. Finally, the warmth from the Sun made the boy remove his cloak and carry it over his arm. This fable shows us that when we use force to control behaviour it doesn't work, like the wind was trying to do, but when we manage behaviour, in the fable the boy made the choice to remove his cloak himself, the outcome is positive. This is a spiritual service to another when we use our wisdom from within to help others.

'We are born from a seed, we grow, we age, we die, we return to the earth and again become the seed that, sooner or later, becomes reincarnate in another person.' Paulo Coelho, Hippie.

An Acorn is as perfect as a fully grown Oak Tree.

HOW TO BE SUCCESSFUL

'Who shall stand in His holy place? He that has clean hands and a pure heart.' Psalms 24:3,4

Swami Umeshranand said the secret of success is to look upon oneself as a spiritual being with a pure and self-luminous nature, eternal within us, the Atman, and assert Its glory when we serve.

This affirmation can help you achieve greater success when you offer your service from your higher self, 'Nothing can interfere with my Divine designed success.'

Our goal in each lifetime is to increase the percentage of Sattva Guna and reduce the levels of Rajas and Tamas Guna, and this occurs when we are successful in our relationships, our careers, our health, our finances, our creativity, talents and in whatever we wish to achieve in life, always doing everything for the benefit of ourselves and others. The higher the level of success the higher the level of Sattva Guna in the samskara for our next lifetime thus paving the way for a more fulfilling life the next time around. This is called, 'The Law of Compensation.'

Action speaks louder than words is a well-known saying because it is a Truth, the good we do for ourselves, and others, is what makes this world a better place. How much good we do or what we do is not the aim here because every act of goodness counts, and the part of the body we use the most doing this good work comes from our hands. The part of our body that is directly linked to the Samskara, our energy field, via the palm chakras. The connection between the samskara, our memory field from many lifetimes, shows up through the physical body in each lifetime in our hands. We use the physical body to assist us in our evolution to higher levels of consciousness, but it is our hands that hold the secret to our evolution, that feeling of success that we achieve in each lifetime comes via the hands. When we create something beautiful using our hands the message to the mind is, 'this is amazing, I did this.' The mind registers it as success and can feel the joy and satisfaction of that activity done by its hands. Our hands give us a greater sense of confidence and courage. When someone is handcuffed, they are restrained, and they feel helpless.

The energy centers in our hands are called chakras or palm chakras and these chakras transmit information from the samskara to the mind and body. These palm chakras balance the seven major chakras in the body, cleanse the auric field, and give power to the hands, and are located just below the ring and little finger. Yogis knew about these palm chakras through their higher wisdom. Today Canadian researchers are telling us that three quarters of the strength in one hand is provided by the ring and little finger. They compared those who had lost fingers due to injury with those who had not. Tests showed those with damage to the ring finger and little finger had a quarter of the strength of those with all five fingers. Their research showed that the ring and little finger provide power to the hand, whilst the other fingers provide dexterity. And scientists say our fingernails are highly sensitive to touch and help us to sense the world around us, and it is the fingernails that allow blind people to localize touch using a cane.

Here is a simple exercise to enhance the sensitivity of your fingertips that you can do with your children, called 'finger racing.' Map out a starting place, and the finish line. Using both hands place the fingertips of the three middle fingers of each hand on the starting line. Have one child as Umpire-when the Umpire says 'Go' make your six fingers, three from each hand, walk as fast as they can to the finish line. First prize goes to the one whose fingers can run the fastest. There is only one rule, fingertips must touch the surface throughout the whole race! The added benefit for this game is that it increases the alertness of the mind.

Our confidence comes from our hands, for example when a small child writes their name for the first time, they feel good about themselves; it is the same with artists, sculptors, musicians, chefs, the creativity that comes from our hands is endless, not to forget the compassion and comfort we can give, or receive, through our hands.

The hands have an unspoken language that all can understand, even for deaf and blind people. Braille is a system of raised dots that can be read with the fingers by people who are blind, and the hands and fingers are used to make signs and shapes so deaf people can understand what someone is saying.

Swami Umeshranand gave me this information, 'The thumbs give us flexibility. The first finger or pointer finger connects us to our intellect and knowledge and gives us a strong will. The middle finger gives us common sense, or the wisdom to get what we need, it enhances our negotiating skills. The ring finger is where our inspiration comes from and is very tuned in to our feelings, it is where most people wear their wedding ring. Yogis say that our ring finger also connects us to the nadis via the samskara and can dissolve negative karma when we touch this finger whilst meditating. The little finger is our source of communication, we use the power in this little finger to know what we want or don't want in life and how we should help others.'

University of California nanoengineer Joseph Wang has created a device that harvests energy from fingertip sweat. The device looks like a foam piece that is attached to an electric circuit connected to a finger pad that creates enough energy to power a small electronic device, like a mobile phone. In other words, our fingers can generate enough energy to charge a mobile phone. We know that fingerprints can unlock a phone or computer but now there are voice graphs that use sound on the fingerprints to determine how long a fingerprint has been at a crime scene. No two fingerprints are alike even if new skin grows the original pattern is duplicated. Our energy flows to a pattern and this pattern are in our hands and is the blueprint for our identity, the person (personality) we are in each lifetime. Who we are is created in the womb (via the samskara) into our hands, and now DNA fingerprinting is proof of this ancient yogi belief. Hello. Countless nursery rhymes and songs have been written for children using their fingers and hands, this was to develop their success by opening these palm chakras.

Every time you place your hands in water imagine these palm chakras opening, because when these chakras are blocked there is a lack of creativity, and we feel shut off from others. These palm chakras are the only chakras that allow us to practice detachment, the head and heart want us to hang on to thoughts that are no longer good for us, but the hands can let them go.

The greater the challenge the bigger the success when we focus on our hands; but our hands also keep us humble, no matter how great our achievements are, when we place them together in prayer position with gratitude.

Do this simple exercise often to keep the hands successful: - Make one tight fist with both hands pressed together, fingers interlocked. Keep making that fist tighter and tighter, now slowly release some of the tightness, release a little more, and a bit more-now stretch the fingers upwards into prayer position, with fingers pressed together, while you focus on your hands for a few moments and bless them.

In the book of Psalms 86-89, when David is anointed King of Israel, he prays to God, "I will walk in thy Truth for thou hast delivered my soul from the lowest hell."

This transformation for David happened via God's hands- 'strong is thy hand and high is thy right hand.' And God gives David power over all of Israel, including the sea and the rivers; 'with whom My hand shall be established; I will set his hand also in the sea and his right hand in the rivers.'

In the book of Job 1:9 the words, "Blessed the work of his hands" refers to the many blessings God had given Job for his faithful service to humanity- a wonderful family, wealth, good health, high standing in the community- all this whilst he was still a young man. Yet in verse 11 Job's faith is tested, via karma, when Satan tells God to take away all that Job has, "put forth thine hand now, and touch all that he has" and Job loses all his blessings; the Sabeans stole his cattle after killing his stockmen; a bush fire destroyed all his sheep, and a band of robbers stole his camels. Then a raging storm blew down the house his children were in and all of them were killed. Yet through all these difficult and heart wrenching experiences, that were karmic, Job stayed faithful to God, and God blesses him with twice as many blessings as he had before, 'And the Lord restored the fortunes to Job, and the Lord gave Job twice as much as he had before.' Through all his hardships Job continued to serve God, because for him it was a sacred service that came from the Sattva Guna that was within him, and he was blessed.

In life it is easier to be happy and helpful when life is rosy and uncomplicated; dealing with chaos and bad luck, (negative karma) will often make people inflict pain on others because they are going through a difficult time. It is at these painful, dark times that we need to let our goodness, light, shine through and continue to serve others and this will allow negative karma to be released so we can be stronger to follow our path of service. Service is sacred action that we offer to our Divine Creator; it is not enough to just be a good role model, we need to be soul models; and then through gratitude and service, we attract more blessings into our life. A person with high levels of Sattva Guna (true virtue) always seeks a way to give, while those with low levels of sattva guna always seeks a way to get.

In Aboriginal Noongar language Doolann means strong hands. Many ancient Aboriginal art works are paintings of hands with the belief that the connectedness of their tribe (mob) was through their hands. In some cultures, just a handshake could seal a deal.

Hindu Brahmins can read a persons' past life and what they have come to accomplish in this life through palmistry. They can tell a person what good they will do in the world in their current lifetime by looking at their hands. They believe that our hands have the power to convey meaning to life and are connected to the energy pattern of the cosmos via the five elements of Earth, Air, Water, Fire and Ether.

Alexander the Great used palmistry to study the lines on his soldiers' hands to analyze their characters. Palmistry was actively suppressed by the Catholic church in the 16th century when they denounced re-incarnation, yet there are references to both in the Bible. Islam also forbids its followers to use palmistry to 'seek knowledge of your fate by divining arrows' Surah Al Mérida 5:3

The Greeks and Romans used hand gestures called Chironomus, and Hindus and Buddhists use the hands to perform sacred rituals called mudras. In yoga, mudras are used to connect with the breath, (our breath stimulates the nerves in our nose whilst also stimulating the nerves in our hands), and the kundalini energy (spiritual) at the base of our spine.

Here is a simple pranayama, yogic breath, that you can do to calm the body and mind after a stressful time: - Put your hands together to form a cup, now place these cupped hands over your mouth and nose and breathe softly. After a few breaths you will feel a lot calmer.

In meditation hand mudras are considered sacred signs to bring the body, mind, and soul into balance. This Mudra, Surya, will improve metabolism and bring balance to your body. Bend your ring finger to the base of your thumb so that your thumb touches the ring finger's knuckle. Stretch your other three fingers straight.

And you can use this other hand mudra to ascend to a higher level of peacefulness as you say this affirmation-

In the portal of light beyond all time.
Grace connects me to the Divine.
I now choose to be free of the past.
In the spirit of truth, I now bask.

Indian classical dance and Thai dances are performed with the hands and fingers and often these dances are stories of past lives and re-incarnation. The Hindu goddess Shakti is usually shown with four or six hands to illustrate her willingness to serve, and the Compassionate Buddha is depicted with a thousand hands, with each hand displaying an all-seeing eye symbolizing sacredness and the wisdom of many lifetimes, with the open palms meaning generosity. Buddhists believe that to develop a compassionate heart the energy that goes from the palm chakra to the heart chakra must be clear and free from all blockages so we can do good deeds. His Holiness, the Dalai Lama says this energy that travels between the two, heart and palm, and from palm to heart, is very important for society and our health. Therefore, they believe hand mudras are sacred.

The Hamsa Hand was believed to have come from the ancient Greeks and Romans and often had an eye symbol in the middle to ward off the evil eye. The Hamsa Prayer:

Let no sadness come to this heart.

Let no trouble come to these arms.

Let no conflict come to these eyes.

Let my soul be filled with the blessing of joy and peace.

In Islam the Hamsa hand symbolizes the Hand of Fatima, the daughter of the Prophet Mohammed. Arabs and Jews in the Middle East raise their hand, five fingers, for good luck and against an evil eye. In the Bible Moses raised his hand and the Israelites destroyed the Amalek in battle. In the Jewish belief the left hand of God delivers justice, and the right hand gives mercy. Psalms 48:10 'Thy right hand is full of righteousness.'

Our service comes via our hands, and for most the right hand is stronger, so we are called to offer service that is right for ourselves and all others.

In the Sistine Chapel in Rome, Italy, there is a famous painting of the creation of humankind depicting the right hand of God stretching out to impact the spark of life from his index finger into Adam's finger.

Many Christians today make the sign of the cross, using their fingers, over the upper part of their body to invoke the blessing of God, by touching their right hand to their forehead, lower chest, and both shoulders. To make the sign of the cross you need to: -

1. Bend the little finger and ring finger into the palm of your right hand.

2. Stretch out the other three fingers with the fingertips touching.
3. Touch your joined fingertips to your forehead.
4. Bring your fingertips down to your abdomen.
5. Move your fingertips to touch the front of your left shoulder.
6. Finally, touch your fingertips to the front of your right shoulder.

The sign of the cross is a sacred ritual performed by Catholic Christians that has links to the city of Fatima.

STORY OF FATIMA

The town of Fatima, named after Mohammed's daughter, is situated in central Portugal. In 1913 an eight-year-old girl, named Lucia dos Santos was looking after a flock of sheep in fields outside the town of Fatima when suddenly she saw a figure hovering above a small oak tree. It was whiter than snow but transparent.

The next year she and her cousins were sheltering in a cave from the rain when they saw the figure Lucia had seen before. It was whiter than snow, but transparent, like crystal. The news of their vision quickly spread and when Lucia got a feeling of going to the oak tree again some fifty people also joined her. The Holy Mother Mary appeared to all of them, and she showed them a vision of her heart and said, "My Immaculate Heart will be your refuge."

In October 1917 almost 80, 000 people joined Lucia when she went to visit the sacred site near the oak tree. What they all witnessed on that day was phenomenal! They saw a vision of the Holy Mother Mary with Joseph and the baby Jesus. Mary and Joseph made the sign of the cross with their right hand and blessed the world. As the vision disappeared Lucia cried out, "Look at the sun."

The sun grew brighter and brighter and suddenly it began to spin round, like a coin spun on its edge. Their faces and bodies were bathed in an intense light. Dr. Jose de Almedia Garrett, a professor at the Faculty of Coimbra was there on that fateful day and wrote an account about it. 'Like everyone else I turned to look at the sun. It was spinning round on itself. I thought that it was remarkable that I could look at it without damaging the retina. Here then we have a miracle witnessed by thousands.'

In the Bible Matthew 8: 14-15 we find these words, 'And when Jesus entered Peter's house, he saw his mother-in-law lying sick with fever; he touched her hand, and the fever left her; and she rose and served him.'

The 'laying on of hands' by the Master Jesus allowed him to heal many people from various illnesses just by placing his hands on them. In Reiki, sacred symbols are drawn, by the hands of Reiki Masters, over a person's body to heal them; and, the initiation process of a Reiki attunement, can release negative karma from a person's samskara.

Reiki originated some 2,500 years ago within the early Buddhist tradition and was re-discovered in Japan by Mikao Usui, who gave the six sacred symbols to a few initiated people to be used in healing. The most complex of all the symbols is used, even today, to clear and heal negative karma. The power of this symbol allows it to dissolve past life negative trauma from the energy field around the body.

Diane Stein in her book, Essential Reiki Teaching Manual says "Almost every serious healing issue, physical or not, is karmic. I feel that the clearing of karma is one of the most crucial issues of our time."

In some religious groups the hand symbolizes the Hand of God and is a sign of protection. In the Book of Esdras 8:7 we read, 'For we are a work of thy hands; thou dost give life to the body, fashioned in the womb, created in fire and water.'

These last words fire, and water, fit in with the Hindu belief that our hands contain the five elements, earth, water, fire, air, and ether within them.

Hand comes from the Greek word 'manus' manifestation, so the ability 'to manifest' is created by the hands. It is our hands that unlock our ultimate success. Open your mind to believing success is in your hands and use your beautiful hands to do good, while we wait for medical evidence to come along and confirm it.

Greg Braden, author of the best-selling book, Human by Design, New Human Story, says that 'Neuroscience breakthroughs are turning conventional brain beliefs on their head.'

He calls them the 'brain lies' that people still believe. I believe we are evolving towards the Truth as the 'unknown' is being revealed more, with new scientific research to back it up.

The Masters of old knew the Truth, but science came along, and everything was disputed due to a lack of evidence, bearing in mind that evidence is only as accurate as the resources available at the time to process it- personal experiences, and an inner wisdom was, and still is, sneered at; but with the massive advances in technology today, designed by people's hands, the unbelievable is becoming believable – our success is in our hands, figuratively and realistically.

SALVATION

Lord, teach me your paths; lead me in your Truth, for you are the God of my salvation.' Psalm 25:4-5'For you Lord are my rock and my salvation--Let no one put me to shame,' Psalm 18:2 The word Salvation is found in most religious texts and is connected to karma and the removal of bad karma, sins, from the samskara.

The book of Zechariah (Bible) is the story of a curse (5:3 & 9:13) that has been passed down to the Israelites for 'threescore and ten years.' (1:12)

For the curse to be lifted the people had to do good deeds in 'truth and righteousness,' "Let your hands be strong, make Jerusalem a city of truth." (8:8,9)

Once the people followed the path of goodness, the curse was replaced with blessings. (9:13)

Thus, in the Song of Zechariah the people are given 'knowledge of salvation by the forgiveness of their sins.' (8:8,9)

This is also the release from the burdens, sins, of our family lineage. In Christianity salvation means being delivered from the penalty of sin, which is eternal death. (Romans 6:23)

Eternal death is many more deaths before all our sins, wrong doings from many lifetimes, are forgiven. (St. John's Gospel 3:15)

The Prophet Ezekiel 36: 22-32 says 'salvation will come in a new body and heart, through the suffering of the servant, till eventually the past is settled and God's salvation will last forever.' In other words, no more re-births.

The word Salvation comes from the Hebrew word Yassa and means to 'set free.' The name Jesus, from the Hebrew name Joshua, means salvation. In the story of the birth of Jesus the Angel tells Mary that she will give birth to a son, conceived of the Holy Spirit, and she is to call him Jesus because he will save his people from their sins. (Matthew 1: 22)

These were the sins of all men, women and children, Jews, and Gentiles, and were related to karma from past life sins, wrongdoings, including the sins they had committed in their present life.

When the Master Jesus began his ministry, he did not just 'save' those people who had done wrong in their present life, but even the sins that had been done in past lives. When Jesus healed the paralytic man (Mark 2:1) he healed him by forgiving his sins, yet there is no mention of the wrongdoing this man had done in his current life, so there is a strong possibility this man's sins had come from a past-life wrong, that Jesus released him from so he could be physically healed.

It was karma from a past life that caused his legs to be paralyzed in his current lifetime. After Jesus cleansed those past life sins his legs were healed, and he could walk. This salvation covers us from all our past, and present lives through karmic opportunities to serve and make past wrongs right. The Bible, especially the New Testament, articulates salvation in terms of past, present, and future time here on earth, leading towards redemption from all sins.

The Prophet Ezra in 2 Esdras 7:59 says, "Choose for yourself life, that you may live." We choose to re-incarnate here lifetime after lifetime till we can finally release all karmic debts and find eternal peace in a Heavenly realm.

In other beliefs, salvation is liberation from negative karma from the samskara, through Self-realization. In Buddhism it is through the realization of Truth that enlightenment and liberation are to be obtained for oneself, through our own efforts, and not by any external help or favour.

Our return to this world again and again is for the evolution of the human Soul to a higher level of consciousness, known in ancient Greek philosophy as the 'Know Thyself' state of being.

This self-realization, the path to salvation, was explained by Patanjali, a sage who lived in India, who translated the yoga sutras from ancient manuscripts that had lain in obscurity for nearly 700 years.

The Aphorisms of Yoga by Shri Patanjali taken from the original version in Sanskrit and explained by Shri Purohit Swami 13,14, 16 and 18.

13. 'In the same way, the three-fold modifications of element and

sense into form, age, and condition can be explained. In the beginning, the forces of the mind are scattered, the yogi tries to knit them together, tries to fix his attention on one object, ultimately finds that both are finally dissolved in the Self. In the same way, elements and sense lose their form. There is clay, the potter reduces it to fine powder, all particles separate from one another, he joins them by some binding material like water, gives it the shape of a vessel, bakes it, uses it, until it is broken, when it is reduced to clay again. In all these stages, it was always clay, nothing but clay, only the form changed. Time is divided into three divisions, which, when reduced, mean only one undivided time. It is all one road, the part of the road that we have travelled is called past, the part of the road that we are travelling is called present, the part of the road that we must travel is called future. In the same way age determines childhood, youth, old age; but there is no age, as there is no time and no form. There is distraction, there is attention, the two fight; concentration is the result. There is ignorance (Tamas), there is passion (Rajas), there is purity (Sattva), the three fight; they have fought before, they are fighting now, they will fight hereafter; in the case of the yogi, he controls them all, attains illumination. It is a fight to the finish. Those who do not carry the fight to a finish are born again and again, they talk of here and hereafter, they talk of past, present, and future, childhood, youth, and age.

14. Substance is that which is uniform in the past, present, and future. The day which we call today, will tomorrow become yesterday; tomorrow will become today after twenty-four hours. Today it is clay, tomorrow it takes the shape of a vessel, the day after it becomes clay again; it is clay all along; it is the substance that remains uniform, though it takes various shapes.

16. Concentrate on the above three-fold modifications, know past and future. The sage Bhrigu worked out sometime in the past the horoscopes of thousands of men, some alive today, some yet to be born. 'I saw my own horoscope, carved on palm leaves, written in Sanskrit, giving an account of my past as well as present life. There are various copies of this collection of horoscopes, I know one which is at Benares, I saw another which belonged to a pundit from Malabar. It is called Bhrigu-Samhita. Generally, three lives are described, or rather one life in the relation to the past and the future life.'

18. Concentrate on the impressions of the past; know past lives.'

In Patanjali's Yoga Sutras cleansing the samskara from high levels of Rajas and Tamas Guna, greed, and ignorance, is achieved when we look within, it is called the redemptive state, when we detach from the material world and focus on self-sacrifice, where we give more and take less.

Patanjali, the great teacher of yoga wrote, 'When freedom from avarice becomes confirmed, the knowledge of the how and wherefore of his previous births comes to the yogi, and by perceiving the impressions of his own mind the yogi comes to have the knowledge of his past life.' Patanjali Yoga Sutras 2:39 (avarice means extreme greed for wealth).

Swami Venkatesananda said, "Patanjali not only gave the world yoga by interpreting the ancient Yoga Sutras he also gave us an understanding of re-incarnation for those who are in search of the truth, which shall free them from self-ignorance."

In Jainism salvation means moksha, release from re-birth and the annihilation of all karma, good and bad, because if karma is still in the samskara it must be cleared in another lifetime.

In Buddhism, salvation is Nirvana, that state of being that is free from all suffering, where the soul finds everlasting peace. Nirvana means 'blown out' as in a candle and refers to the blowing out of the fire of desire, Rajas guna, of all aversion and delusion, when the darkness of ignorance, Tamas guna, transmutes into the light of liberation, Sattva guna. In Buddhism someone who reaches nirvana but still chooses to return to earth to alleviate suffering in the world is called a Bodhisattva because they are filled with the goodness of Truth.

In Tantra yoga Dharma, sacred service, brings the devotee's mind to the realization of the Truth so that enlightenment and liberation can be obtained for oneself and by oneself through our own effort.

Some Christians refer to the 'born again' experience. This is often a process of releasing past wrongs and starting a new life by becoming more spiritual and God conscious through salvation. In re-incarnation it literally means just that – born again.

For Muslims salvation comes with repentance. "In the end, to your Lord is your return, when He will tell you the truth of all that ye did in this life." Quran Sura 39:32

The Prophet Mohammed said, "I seek repentance from Him a hundred times a day." Sahih Muslim 35:65

James Akin, a Catholic theologian said, "I have been saved, I am being saved, and I will be saved."

This saved, salvation, is from karma, that only the Divine energy of light can give us, it is the release of all negative/dark energy.

Travelling through the State of Alabama in the U.S. I saw many signs on cars and churches referring to salvation, like this one 'Are You Saved?' 'If Not, Why Not?'

One church Ken and I attended the Minister got us to repeatedly say 'I am a sinner' again and again, louder, and louder. I thought to myself, 'it must be from our past lives,' because I am sure most of us sitting there were good people even if we had made a few mistakes along the way in our current life.

Our self-development continues in each lifetime, as we are given opportunities to feel compassion and empathy for all people so we cannot hurt another. What moves you to tears? If its from your Soul it's called compassion, if it comes from your ego, it's called self-pity.

Why do we feel fear, pain, and suffering more strongly than we feel safe, wellness, and joy? Why do we feel the lost love, more than the love we have now?

Because over time we have allowed our feelings of negative experiences to become stronger by not letting them go. The longer we hang on to those bad experiences, the more power we give them, to the point where they can control our lives in this lifetime and in the next, because over time they develop into self-pity.

I was talking to a woman who had three beautiful children, yet she constantly felt sad over the baby she had miscarried. Enlightenment is the quiet acceptance of what is.

Our feelings respond to our memories, even those from our past lives, even when we cannot consciously recall them.

Recently on National Television the Duchess of Sussex, Meghan Markle made a comment to Oprah Winfrey, a well-known American television presenter, that when she was pregnant with her first child a member of the Royal Family had made a racist remark about what skin-colour her child would be born with. This racist remark was emotionally distressing to the Duchess because it felt painful to her. This reaction is karmic because it is coming from deep within the memory field. When we re-act strongly to any comment made to us by another person it is because it has been done to us before and the memory of that emotional hurt is in the samskara. In Meghan Markle's case this newest racial comment re-ignited the spark that was already there, and the emotional pain returned. Overlooking it or dismissing it is not an option because it has never been addressed and healed. There are many ways in which it could have materialized in the samskara, it could have happened before she was born whilst still in her mother's womb, science tells us that babies feel and hear things in the womb, or someone could have made a racist remake to her in her early childhood, or the memory could have come from a past life experience? This is where the practice of detachment is most beneficial, by letting the negative feeling go, and replacing it with a positive one, such as 'my child is a beautiful, caring human being who is deeply loved' replaces the old negative memory of pain or shame into a positive memory of having a beautiful baby.

Here is a simple breathing exercise called The Breath of Life to release bad memories from this lifetime and other lifetimes:

Lie down and imagine that you are surrounded by a pure white light, and breathe deeply into your belly, pushing your belly right up.

As you exhale let your negative thoughts dissolve into the light around you.

Breathe in again, all the way to the belly and say, "I connect to the Universal Divine Light around me."

Exhale dissolving the negative karma into the Light around you.

Feel each inhale and exhale as you do this at least 5 times.

Some yogis believe this big belly breath can even change our DNA, because it aligns our auric field, samskara, with the Universal light grid, or the Life Force energy. Science is now telling us there is evidence showing a link between our genes, our DNA, and our second brain in our gut, that was known by yogis thousands of years ago.

When we connect to the Universal Light frequency, that Christians refer to as the Christ Light, we can heal karmic wounds from the past, as we fully align to our highest Truth and purity.

The Master Jesus told his followers, "The Truth will set you free." (John 8:32)

In the sacred Hindu book, the Bhagavad Gita 2:16, we read this –

'The unreal never is. The real never is not.

Men possessed of the knowledge of the Truth fully know both these.'

The Master Jesus put it like this, 'the spirit is willing, but the flesh is weak.' (Matthew 26: 41)

The truth is, the power of spirit is far greater than the human mind, and a spiritual experience is far greater than a human experience because the depth of feelings is more intense.

Everyone is out there searching for something, but the buck stops with us – the answers are within, it is our deepest thoughts that contain all our answers to life.

Scientists have discovered phosphine gas on Venus' upper cloud deck, about 62km above its surface. This gas is produced by animals that live in oxygen-free environments. Professor Alan Duffy from the Royal Institution of Australia is thrilled with the find saying, "this is one of the most exciting signs of the possible presence of life beyond Earth I have ever seen."

The Masters of old knew there was life beyond earth with their inner knowing. But for those seeking evidence science is proving these esoteric truths. Experiments being carried out now are making what was believed to be impossible before possible, especially when it comes to our own bodies and mental capabilities. Australian scientists and surgeons have given patients with disabilities the power to work on a computer with their mind.

Professor Peter Mitchell said the sky was the limit now they had proved disabled people had the ability to translate thought into action and "the limits of what can be achieved, we just don't know."

We are so much more than what we believe ourselves to be, especially when we add all our experiences from our past lives. And each time someone says, "that won't work," and someone 'brave' enough to do so carries on till it does work we are all amazed, even though we shouldn't be because this wisdom has been with us forever.

At New York's Museum of Modern Art Marina Abramovic asked the curator if she could sit on a chair for 8 hours a day and be allowed to have an empty chair opposite for any visitors to sit on so she could converse silently with their soul.

The curator told her people were too busy, no one had time to simply sit and stare! But nonetheless he gave her the opportunity. Each day people waited hours to sit with Marina; there were lines out the door. Some came back multiple times to connect with 'themselves.' Marina met the souls of 1,565 people in that time. She said that when all inhibitions melt away there is only two sets of eyes and a sense of 'nothingness.' For some people just sitting there gazing into another's eyes made them aware of their own vulnerability. Some had feelings so strong they began to cry. Marina explained it as an opportunity to look at oneself through the eyes of another. She called it "the fullness in space between two souls."

It has been said that 'the eyes are the windows to the soul.'

You can judge how a person is feeling by looking into their eyes. In some cultures, looking directly into a person's eyes was unacceptable, because it was considered disrespectful. Whilst others viewed it as rudeness not to look at a person when being spoken to. As each person learns to stand in their own power, they will 'see' that making eye contact is a way of expressing how they are feeling.

This simple exercise will allow you to look at your soul light:

Light a candle and softly gaze into the flame.

Give it your full focus, there is only you and the candle flame.

Keep looking at the candle flame for as long as you can.

Now close your eyes.

Open your eyes again and gaze into the flame and this time lift your eyes upwards, eyelids slightly down, and you will see hazy strands of light coming from your third eye moving towards the candle. This is the light coming from your Soul.

The strong rays of light coming from the candle will be coming towards your heart, whilst the hazy, wispy strands of light will be moving away from your head towards the candle.

Stay looking at your soul light and the rays of the candlelight for as long as you can.

Now close your eyes and feel a deep connection between your heart and soul.

Recently a famous Australian swimmer lost her daughter to an eating disorder. For many years, the family did everything they could to help her. Each time she improved their hopes grew. But then she would re-lapse and the worry and fears returned, till her body ran out of strength and gave up.

A relative of mine went through the same painful journey of anorexia with her daughter. Nothing they tried had a lasting effect, because each time their daughter would return to trying to starve herself. My relative went and saw a psychic/medium who told her that her daughter had suffered starvation in a concentration camp during the second world war and that the memory of that starvation in a past life was so strong her mind was repeating the process in this life. Nobody will ever know whether that story changed her daughter's way of thinking but after that information her daughter never denied her body from having food again. It could be the same for those who over-eat, but in reversal. From being starved in a past-life, due to a lack of food, to over-indulgence because they now have access to unlimited food.

Today new scientific techniques to help overcome excessive body weight are working with the unconscious beliefs, and traumas, from within the body, that stop some people from losing weight. No longer do therapists send their clients home with just a good eating plan. Research now shows there is more to the overweight problems than just bad eating habits.

Often our strongest memories are the most painful ones, because these are the ones we feel the most. People with addictions in this life can almost certainly return in another lifetime with the same addiction or cravings. People who die from a drug overdose or alcohol abuse would remember that last craving, or overwhelming desire for a drink or for drugs before they died, and that craving, or desire, would be firmly embedded in their samskara.

In their next life as soon as alcohol or drugs entered their body that strong memory would be triggered and slipping into that addictive behaviour would be hard to control or stop.

According to Swami Umeshranand our addictions are not caused by genetics, or copying adults, or parent behaviour, but through a powerful memory of wanting (craving) a drink or drugs that is in the samskara because the levels of Rajas Guna (desire and greed) are high. 'Unknown to the deluded being is the wicked reign of karma, seeping into the being-into every cell, pre-determining how a cell, an organ or an individual behaves, controlling every breath, thought and emotion. Untold despair befalls the seeker as he realizes one day that his most prized 'freedom' is but a complex function of the karmic influences from the past.' Sadhguru

Nearly all religious traditions have a form of cleansing the 'sins' (karma) of babies soon after birth. In the Christian religion it is called Baptism. From the 3rd. century onwards many Christians baptized infants to cleanse all their preceding sins. They believed all children were born with a fallen human nature and tainted by original sin, so to be freed from the power of darkness the ritual purification of baptism was performed, and that signified liberation from sin. Some babies were baptized on the second or third day after they were born. Where could they have collected all these sins from? At this young age they were unable to do wrong. Yet the holy prayer started like this: "Almighty and ever living God we pray for this child, set him (her) free from original sin."

In Catholic tradition the holy Mother Mary was born without sin and Catholics say this prayer to acknowledge this belief 'O Mary, conceived without sin, pray for us, who have recourse to Thee.' Yet the belief amongst Christians is that Jesus died to free all from original sin, so why the need to remove sins from each new baby?

The truth is that the ritual cleansing of a baby's sins at baptism was, and still is, a cleansing of past life negative karma.

The Lutherans took it even further believing babies were conceived and born sinful, indicating low levels of Sattva Guna. And in some Roman Catholic churches the baptism ceremony took on the form of an exorcism ritual where the priest wanted to remove Satan from inside the child. Some Orthodox Christian churches give infants consecrated bread and wine after baptism to cleanse them from their sins. All these practices were carried out as cleansing rituals in the Christian church yet re-incarnation and collecting bad karma from past lives was not believed, which is still not a belief in many Christian churches today.

Hindus, Buddhists, Jains, Sikhs, and many other faiths all believe in re-incarnation, as do a lot of tribal people.

In Tibetan Buddhism the Dalai Lama is chosen from a child who was a previous Dalai Lama. According to their beliefs a new Dalai Lama, or spiritual leader, can only be chosen by evidence or signs of them being a previous Dalai Lama. People heard the 16th Lama singing Om Mani

Padme Hum, the most sacred of all the mantras, whilst he was still in his mother's womb. Whilst young he showed remarkable understanding of the Buddhist Scriptures and was able to read and write from the age of 2! He even remembered people and places from his previous incarnations.

The first Dalai Lama was born in 1390. He started from humble beginnings, being born in a cattle pen, like the Master Jesus who was born in a stable. Tibetan Buddhists believe this same Soul had been re-incarnated 14 times, though the Kadapa teachings go as far back as 980 with previous incarnations, in a lineage that can be traced back to a Brahmin boy who lived at the same time of Buddha Shakyamuni. What they all had in common was an amazing ability to re-call memories from their past lives around the ages of two and three that proved to the holy leaders that they were indeed holy men in their past life whose Soul had come back to continue their work of service in a new body.

These wise teachers, lamas, return to earth with a high percentage of Sattva Guna, goodness, and low levels of Rajas Guna, greed, and Tamas Guna, ignorance. They return each lifetime to serve humbly and cheerfully whilst sharing their wisdom; the current Dalai Lama smiles a lot. They have overcome ignorance, cravings, and attachments, the roots of negative karma that most people find hard to change.

Swami Umeshranand would say, "If one gets the seed of devotional service and cultivates it, that person becomes free from the cycle of birth and death. One constructive act can change the effects, karma, of many destructive acts, as the unstable thoughts and addictions start to dissolve."

As we open our consciousness to understanding our true purpose for being here, that is to serve, the esoteric mysteries of re-incarnation and karma will become more acceptable to our way of thinking and believing. Death for all of us would then become a preparation for our return, and a chance to become enlightened souls, till finally the choice is ours, to return, or not, to this earthly realm.

The poet Robert Frost says this perfectly:

'The woods are lovely, dark, and deep,

but I have promises to keep,

and miles to go before I sleep.'

Karma is our own doing, from each lifetime of experiences, reacting on ourselves. Our aim in each lifetime is the final destruction of ALL karma. How we respond to each challenging experience, how well we cope in every situation without hurting others or becoming a burden to others, creates good or bad karma. Giving others love and support is healing and produces good karma but hurting or blaming another for things that do not go according to one's plans is not constructive, it is destructive, and because our time is limited on earth, we need to move forward, not wait until we run out of time to do the good deeds we have come here to do.

Morris Netherton, who did many Past Life Regressions described karma as 'a debt to us, to be repaid by us, at a time we choose, and, by the way we choose.'

In the big picture our time here is short, even if we live past 100. Age isn't just a number, it's an attitude too that has developed over a long period of time from our beliefs. It is never too late to serve; what we leave behind is what counts. I have heard of a lady who is 94 who loves to cook so cooks' soup for the homeless that volunteers pick up from her home every day. And in an aged care home women there knit tiny beanies for pre-mature babies in a women's public hospital.

When we use our age to stop helping others, we are denying ourselves from using our soul energy. Remember our soul is ageless. Doing anything good for humanity and supporting others through our interaction with them is crucial to healing ourselves and the world.

Some people think by giving donations they have done their good deeds this time around, but the giving of one's energy is more important, because this is true compassion, it is our interaction with others that counts the most, how do we make people feel about themselves? Are we giving them their power back, or are we taking it away from them?

A relative of mine saw a homeless man on the street asking for money to buy food so she asked him if he would like to clean up her yard and she would pay him. He accepted her offer and after three hours of working she paid him, and she felt a change in his attitude towards himself because she had given him the opportunity to give as well as receive.

Some people hold fund-raising events where many people get together to share food or items and the money collected is given to charity. This is sharing our energy and money whilst doing good. Hindus call this selfless action. Christians call it unconditional love. Buddhists call it compassion.

We can forgive, but forgetting is impossible, because the memory cannot be deleted from the samskara, but when we forgive, the memory in the samskara loses its pain, and this is crucial in healing a past, or recent, memory. Then when we reflect on the experience at a deeper level, we feel the pain less, and the memory of that painful experience weakens in the samskara, till eventually there is no feelings at all when that memory is re-called. It has become a little ripple in a stream of water that does not hurt or distress us when we remember that experience. Like physical pain, it can hurt badly when first inflicted, then once healing happens, even though the memory of that pain from the injury is still there, that pain would no longer be strong enough to feel.

That is how it is with karmic pain – we might not have any conscious memory of being abused, or hurt, yet we can feel other people's pain when hearing of their abuse. In our case it is a feeling from a past life memory triggered by another's experience. We are connected to each other by how we felt at the time of that painful experience, regardless of when it occurred.

The writer Humphreys said.

Sow a thought, reap an act.

Sow an act, reap a habit.

Sow a habit, reap a destiny.

And according to Shri Aurobindo from the Aurobindo Ashram in Pondicherry, India, where professors have studied re-incarnation in great depth, "Our fate and our temperament have been built by our own wills and our own wills can alter them."

Our past life experiences affect how we live today, but we can lighten the darker memories when we actively engage in using the 'light' energy from our energy centers called chakras, that resonate within the body. If you have never done work with your chakra energy before, then this is a good time to begin.

Do this exercise every day for 365 days. If you miss one day, do it twice the next, but do not miss doing it because repetition creates a belief, and a belief becomes your reality.

You will need to have seven pieces of coloured material with you when you do this exercise, red, orange, yellow, green, light blue, dark blue (indigo) and purple.

Now looking at the red colour place your hand just below your belly button and say, 'I believe in myself.'

Now look at the orange colour and place your hand on your belly button and say, 'I develop emotional self-mastery.'

Look at the yellow colour and place your hand above your belly button and say, 'I follow my intuition.'

Gaze at the green colour and place your hand on your heart and say, 'I follow my heart.'

Look at the light blue colour and place your hand on the spot where you can feel the hollow in your throat and say, 'I align to my truth.'

Place the dark blue colour on your forehead, over your third eye (the spot between your eyebrows), and say, 'I see the BIG picture,'

Place the purple colour on your head, slightly to the back, and imagine that purple colour filling your mind and say, 'I tune into my Soul.'

At the end of the 365 days, you will believe in the subtle energies of the chakras and now you can use each chakra and its associated colour to heal negative experiences from your samskara.

For example, if you are afraid or embarrassed to speak up about an injustice surround yourself with the colour light blue, look up to the sky and keep saying, 'I align to my truth.' You will get the courage and confidence to speak up and you will do it wisely. This wisdom has come from many lifetimes and is there within you to use when necessary. Just as the perfect blueprint of the oak tree is in the acorn, the blueprint of our life for each lifetime is in the Samskara, and we can access this wisdom through the super conscious mind, or spiritual mind, whenever we need too.

'Wisdom grows as gently as an oak tree and lives as long a life.'

Along with the Tree of Wisdom, to the Celts the oak tree was also the Tree of Truth, and this wisdom and truth is in the consciousness of all people as it is in the acorn, the seed from which the oak tree grows.

To the Celts the oak tree was the guardian of history (memories), and endurance.

In Lincolnshire, U.K. there is an oak tree 1,500 years old.

In Sanskrit the oak is Duir, meaning spiritual gateway to the past, present, and future.

Today in some countries the oak is used on the badges of the armed forces as a symbol of service, which is our purpose for coming here again and again-we are here to serve.

The symbol of the tree has been used since the beginning of time to create that link between humankind and the sacred realms. Buddha received enlightenment sitting under a Bodhi tree, and the 8 limbs of yoga is depicted on the Tree of Life. This Tree of Life is so sacred it is regarded as the source of eternal life in many religions.

The Family Tree, that is becoming very popular amongst people today, has no link to karma and re-incarnation. It is a modern distraction for those interested in finding out who their great-great-great grandparents were, forgetting that our soul is older than any Family Tree and that our great-great grandparents from this lifetime might not have had any connection with us in any of our past lives whatsoever, so why check it out?

W.Y. Evans-Wentz in his book, Tibetan Yoga and Secret Doctrines, that was first published in 1935 says 'In a biological sense man is today literally the heir of all the ages. If the Oriental sages be right, man has been and will be, in a way yet unsuspected by our biologists, his own ancestor.'

Many of our present-day phobias are connected to past life trauma and has nothing to do with our ancestry. Sometimes we do go back into families we had a past life with, and sometimes we do not. It depends on what the Soul needs, to evolve, in each lifetime.

Vivekananda, the great Indian sage who was Sri Ramakrishna greatest disciple said "There is something in us which is free and permanent. But it is not the body, neither is it the mind. The body is dying every minute. The mind is constantly changing. The body is a combination, and so is the mind, and as such can never reach a state beyond all change. But beyond this momentary sheathing of gross matter, beyond even the finer covering of the mind is the Atman, the true Self of man, the permanent, the ever free. It is his freedom that is percolating through layers of thought and matter, and despite the colourings of name and form, is ever asserting Its unshackled existence. It is His deathlessness, His bliss, His peace, His divinity, that shines out and makes Itself felt despite the thickest layers of ignorance. He is the real Man, the fearless One, the deathless One, the Free-----his Being, this Atman, the real Self of man the Free, the Unchangeable, is beyond all conditions and as such it has neither birth nor death. Without birth or death, eternal, ever existing is the Soul of man." (The Complete Works, Vol. 1 pg. 124)

This Soul of wisdom, our higher consciousness, gives us the truth and allows us to reflect on everything that we do in life. Our interaction with others must reflect our desire to help them, even if at times we say, or do, the opposite to what the other person is expecting. The Sattva Guna in our samskara is always guiding us to do what is right. Remember we have many lifetimes of experience under our belt! Age does not create wisdom, its lifetimes. Some kids are smarter than adults because they can tap into their many lifetime experiences. How often do we hear people say, 'this one has been here before," when referring to a young child?

Have you ever done something and then been amazed how well it turned out? This inner wisdom can only come when the level of ignorance, Tamas-Guna, is of a low percentage in your samskara.

The samskara is part of our etheric body, it is part of us, people look for answers outside of them, but it comes from within. The eternal nature of our Soul gives us a broader understanding of our current incarnation.

Practicing yoga and meditation are excellent ways of going within when dealing with karmic experiences. Sometimes our challenges come to us one after the other. The first couple might be easy to deal with, but as they start to pile up, we are left exhausted, and we feel a sense of hopelessness and can wonder if all the effort is worth it. Yes, it is, because remember we become more powerful when we do not quit or resort to becoming aggressive or withdrawn. Yes, we can call time out, but this should only be a short-term solution, any longer makes us reclusive and then we could feel isolated and alone in this life and our next life. We humans are sociable creatures, our interaction with others gives us the feeling of love and belonging; without it we become cold and resentful towards others for excluding us- but to have a friend we need to be a friend.

Karma is our own doing reacting on ourselves. Our aim through our many lifetimes here on earth is the final destruction of all karma, to manifest the pure soul. Sometimes when we experience a moment of higher spiritual consciousness, we can get a glimpse of our pure Soul.

On a trip to Sedona in Arizona I went to visit the Chapel of the Holy Cross, a beautiful Christian Chapel cut into the rocks that surround Sedona. It was quite a climb up to the Chapel, that had been built by a woman in memory of her mother. From miles away the large cross in front of the altar could be seen. Inside the Chapel it was serene and still and sitting on the pew bench I felt a sense of holiness as I gazed at the cross and the light, that was streaming in through the large windows, high up on that mountain. As I was descending the long flight of steps going down, I was zapped, it was like I had touched an electric- wire but it was an extraordinarily nice feeling. At first, I was not quite sure what had happened to me. For the next three days I did not want to eat, I drank water and because my husband was getting concerned about me, I ate a piece of fruit. Nor did I sleep for three days, I just felt energized; there was no tiredness in my body. I mentioned my experience to a fellow traveler, who then explained to me the vortexes that were around Sedona.

There are four main energy vortexes in Sedona. The subtle energy that exists at these locations interacts with a person's kundalini energy, or soul energy. It resonates with and strengthens the Inner Being of each person that comes within about 250 meters of it. This connection occurs because the vortex energy is like the subtle energy that is within the energy centers of each person. If a person is at all sensitive to these subtle energies it is easy to feel the energy in these vortexes. Absorbing energy in this way can have a positive effect on you for days afterwards. People go to Sedona from all over the world to experience this energy.

The energy from those vortexes made my thinking clearer, it was like I had received more clarity to the answers of life, and more insight into the energy field of the samskara and past life experiences. I also believe it released some of the negative energy from within my samskara, because it felt like an internal cleansing.

Whilst in Sedona I went to a workshop given by Denise Linn who told us her story of being shot when she was a teenager.

One day whilst she was riding her bike home from school, she heard a car coming behind her, so she moved off the road onto the dirt path along the side of the road, but the car went off the road and hit her and knocked her off her bike and drove off. She managed to get herself up but was not sure if her bike was in any condition for her to be able to ride it, when she noticed the car turn around and come towards her. She thought the driver must have noticed her fall off her bike and was returning to make sure she was ok, but instead he lent out of his window and shot her and drove off. Another car came along a bit later and found her lying on the side of the road, in a bad way, and took her to hospital where they found that the bullet had gone right through her body and lodged into her spine. The surgeons told her she would never walk again, but she did, although it was a long and slow journey to getting back on her feet again.

What Denise told us at the workshop made perfect sense to me because she said it was karmic debt that made the man shoot her in this lifetime. Her acute esoteric wisdom had allowed her to feel and understand the real meaning behind that shocking experience. Even her daughter was a blessing when she was told she would never have children, because she refused to be a victim of karma. She accepted her karmic experiences that enabled her to live a happy and successful life. Denise's story is an example of strength and perseverance that came from within.

Johann Wolfgang Van Goethe, 1820, said 'There are but two roads that lead to an important goal and to the doing of great things: strength and perseverance. Strength is the lot of a few privileged people, but austere perseverance, harsh and continuous, may be employed by the smallest of us.'

Swami Umeshranand called this type of experience, like Denise's, Karmic enmeshment – entanglement with another soul that has its roots in past lives in which karma, or actions, are repeated.

In 1995 in Perth, Western Australia, a man murdered his ex-wife by suffocating her, but before he killed her, he made her write a letter to their children. Here is part of that letter – ' I am writing this letter at your father's insistence. I have just been told I am going to be killed. I don't want to die and funny enough I don't hate your dad even now. All I can say is I feel so much for all of us. Please stand by each other and give each other strength-be there for each other and do not blame anything or anyone, for blame is hate. I really don't hate. I love you, Mum.'

The man's attempt at suicide failed and he was jailed for life. Here then is another true story of karmic enmeshment.

When I stayed in Darjeeling, India, I visited the Bhutia Busty Monastery, that began as a simple bamboo structure near a rock cave in the year 1600, to hide the teachings of Buddha that were written on yak scrolls. These sacred scrolls, hidden in a tunnel in the rock, were shown to me by an old monk using a flashlight because no one could touch them. The trip there was interestingly unnerving, because I got caught in a cloud, I was literally standing in a cloud for about 10 minutes unable to see or hear anything. Quite eerie especially as I was next to a protected state forest where wild animals like black panthers, Bengal tigers, and wolves and other animals roam freely! Whilst standing nervously in the cloud I did regret not getting onto the mule the Nepali woman kept trying so hard to convince me to ride on, for the trip to Bhutia Busty Monastery. Anyway, the cloud lifted, and all was well and the sights on my walk were breathtakingly beautiful, as was the monastery; such a spiritually transforming moment and Lama Thupten smiled a lot. But the most valuable gift I received on my visit was a sacred mantra from the oldest monk living there-Om Baja Shatu Ho-to remove the darker energies of karmic enmeshment.

Some years later Swamiji Umeshranand explained to me the ritual of Japa, through visualization, to remove past life karmic enmeshment from hurting us in this lifetime. 'Visualization on the holy Personality, Deity, serves as the connecting link between the Finite and the Infinite and understood this way it satisfies the head and the heart. Japa means calling up the image of the Deity, whether it be Christ or Buddha or Krishna; this holy form must be visualized as luminous and blissful, and living and real. Think of yourself as luminous and then install the luminous form of your Chosen Ideal in the luminous center at the region of the heart. The mantra, sound, is a symbol of Divinity, the Form also is a symbol of Divinity. We take the help of both the symbols to call up the Divine Consciousness then the bad karma cannot affect us anymore.'

This mantra, Om Baja Shatu Ho, when chanted continuously whilst focusing on any chosen Deity, is the sacred ritual of Japa that can remove negative karmic enmeshment.

The oak sleeps in the acorn

The bird waits in the egg,

And the soul waits for moksha (no more re-birth)

'Knowing that Christ, being raised from the dead dieth no more, death hath no more dominion over him.' Romans 6:9

The highest vision of the Soul is release from all bad karma, or spiritual debt, that accumulates from all previous lives and this life

Each lifetime is a lifetime of service to humanity, the type of work we do is irrelevant when it is for the welfare of others. This service also calls us to help others not to collect bad karma. For example, if someone is in a violent, toxic, relationship and they accept that bad behaviour from their partner by saying or doing nothing about it, from fear, or shame, because of what others will think of their relationship, are allowing their violent partner to collect more bad karma, whilst also collecting bad karma for themself, because they are condoning this type of violence and abuse. Our passiveness also collects bad karma when the actions are wrong, and we turn a blind eye to it. It is important to speak up and seek help to make a wrong right. This is service to humanity and will bring good karma

A friend in the family has a brother who is a drug dealer. One day his brother came home and found his son had hung himself. He called one of his associates and told him to take the body away and arrange the funeral. All three people have collected karmic debt. As tragic as it was for the boy who took his own life, it still gave him bad karma because he did not work hard enough to change or move away from that toxic environment, and for the father who was a drug dealer and made his money by destroying other people's lives, and for the person who carried out the orders, if he was part of the drug dealing scheme.

This is the same for people who think they are helping their adult children when they give them food and shelter only to be constantly abused by them. Everyone here is increasing their karmic debt for their next life.

Service calls for making people into better human beings- more humble, more grateful, more compassionate, and more considerate. Helping someone to become more selfish, more verbally or physically abusive, or accepting their lies, because calling out their lies will upset them, is blocking you from collecting good karma, even though you might think you are helping that person. This kind of service has no value in the law of karma.

Swami Umeshranand asked me what unconditional love meant to me? I said it was showing and giving love in all situations. And he said that was not the TRUTH.

He said the heart is sacred and love is sacred, and we honour it and hold it within all its purity, it was not to be dispatched without sincerity. He said that the sharing of the gift of love was so sacred it should only be shared with honesty and trust and integrity. Giving it away as some cheap commodity made the interpretation of love insipid. He said people needed to earn our love, so they could respect it. He said our love should inspire others to do better. Other than that, it was merely a word that was being loosely thrown around, and sometimes it was done to make you 'look' better, a case of "I will still love you, no matter what you do." He said, "Are you telling someone who has just raped a small child that you love them regardless of their evil actions? Do you honestly love them from your heart of hearts? Of course you do not, you loathe them instead, so your lies will not accumulate any good karma for you."

Swami Umeshranand said love had to be sincere, and according to him most people did not understand that depth of sincerity. Love without sincerity was merely mouthing words. He said people who worked with light, and love and goodness understood detachment. Detachment is when we respond rather than re-act to each situation in the name of service.

When we serve, we do it to help people on their life path so they can help others. There is no other motive. Some people believe they will love them into being better people, but for those individuals who are not working with light and goodness, they will simply take that energy of love you have so freely given and use it to do more harm and destruction. And the more love and kindness shown to them the more selfish and demanding they will become, to the point that no matter how much you give them, or how much you do for them, it will never be enough.

To cleanse bad karma, we need to serve where our service is valued. Accepting abuse in the hope that one day our service will be valued is called wasting time, remember our time here is short, there is no time to waste or spend collecting negative karma, because it is going to take so much longer to clear in the next lifetime. The only solution is to detach from these people physically and emotionally.

The sacred Hindu text of the Garuda Purana says, 'Quit the country, and people, where you can find neither friends or joy, nor in which is there any knowledge to be gained.' 109:40

A friend of mine in India gave accommodation to two men who were alcoholics, they got money through begging. When I stayed at her home, I felt an instant dislike towards those two men, and as hard as I tried to overcome it the feeling persisted. They lived in a storeroom behind the house and at night I would hear the most pitiful howling and noises of distress coming from the stray dogs near that storeroom. I know they were doing despicable things to those animals, that they would entice with scraps of food. I reported them to the police, but I doubt if anything was done, because at that time animal cruelty was not taken seriously in India, so it was not an offence. What my friend saw as an act of kindness was in truth an opportunity for those two men to indulge in their deviant behaviour and collect more bad karma. Their suffering in their next life will be even greater unless they return and offer honourable service to people and animals.

When we offer our service to others, we need to give it so that they too can return that service to others and live a good life. It is a form of 'pay it forward.' If, after a good amount of time invested in them does not pay off, then it is time to help someone else, because when giving allows some people to inflict more suffering on others then your help is also creating bad karma for you. Our aim in service must always be to help others become better human beings, more compassionate, more grateful and humble. This is called virtuous service and bestows good karma on all.

Another friend of mine was married to a man who verbally and physically abused her for 10 years, she believed if she kept showing him love and kindness, he would change but giving him all the love from her heart and trying to keep him happy did not change the way he treated her. Finally, she left him, knowing that all the love in the world was not going to change him for the better. By doing this she gave both of themselves the opportunity to create good karma, away from each other.

'A gift, made at a proper time and place, to a deserving person, in a true spirit of compassionate sympathy, carries the merits of all sorts of pious acts.' Garuda Purana chapter 93:35

Dr. Denis Waitley said, "There are two primary choices in life: to accept conditions as they exist or accept the responsibility for changing them."

Our aim must always be to collect good karma for this and our next life.

Remember each one of us come to this life with the 3 modes of impressions in our samskara, so trying to reform someone who has returned to this life with a high percentage of Rajas Guna, that gives them an unhealthy desire to hurt others, and hoping to change it into Sattva Guna might take many lifetimes, so do not lower your own levels of Sattva Guna by unintentionally aiding them in increasing their levels of Rajas Guna.

The Master Jesus, (Matthew 10:14) instructed his disciples to turn away from people who would not accept their good counsel and help and to move on to other people who respectfully listened to their words of wisdom and gratefully accepted their help. He took it even further in how to distance themselves from such negative people by telling them to leave even the dust behind from that place that might have stuck to their sandals. In other words, Jesus instructed his followers to make a clean break away from those people.

The Master Jesus wanted his disciples' service to be valuable and transforming.

In the Bible, Luke chapter 17:2, Jesus said these words: "Offences will come, but woe unto him through whom they come! It is better for him that a millstone was hanged about his neck, and he was cast into the sea, than he should offend one of these little children." What Jesus was saying in this Biblical verse relates to karma, that sometimes it is better to exit this life, than to keep creating more bad karma.

Research has shown that it is difficult for pedophiles to reform, and the likelihood of them returning to sexually abusing children, even after a prison sentence, is highly probable.

At the last supper that Jesus had with his disciples, just before his crucifixion, he would have known that one of his disciples, Judas, was about to betray him because in Mark 14:1 he says, "For the son of man goes as it is written of him, but woe to that one by whom the son of man is betrayed! It would have been better for that one not to have been born." This is an indication of the negative karma Judas received by his act of betrayal, which he did for money, greed, by increasing the level of Rajas guna in his samskara.

Our service in each lifetime must be to bring the light of God into each soul and the purity of God into their feelings. Our goal is not to impress others but to inspire others. Our service should inspire others to do better.

From the Buddhist book, The Practices of Kindness we read, 'Unless we give what we have to others, what we know, and value will be irrevocably and utterly gone.'

We can get bogged down trying desperately to help one person into becoming a better human being and then find out nothing has changed within themselves; or we can move on, detach from that person, and help ten other people in that space of time. Where will good karma come from? Helping the one who never improved? Or helping the 10 who moved forward and became better people?

There are some people who adamantly believe that love will transform everyone and everything, but people who hurt others and feel no remorse or empathy for their victims do not deserve our love and support, but they do need our prayers to heal their behaviour. Give love and support to the innocent victims, and this will empower them to make better choices in their life. From the New Testament Bible, 1 John 3: 18 come these words, 'Let us not love with words or speech but with actions and in truth.'

Sincere love builds good karma and so does honest anger.

In all the research I have done on positive and negative karma I have never come across anything that says anger is bad. Some yogis believe that expressing anger, without violence, is good karma because it lets us be truly honest. Even the Master Jesus vented out his anger at the traders who violated the sacred space of the synagogue. Matthew 21:12-17

Thinking of those people who shot down that Malaysian Airlines plane that was on its way from Amsterdam to Kuala Lumpur over eastern Ukraine on July 17, 2014, with 283 passengers and 15 crew on board and experiencing a feeling of anger towards the people responsible for bringing that plane down justifies our anger because it shows that we have an awareness of right and wrong and we are aware of the wrong that was done. We know what is right and what is wrong from within. Feeling that anger towards the Russian and Ukraine men who fired off that missile into the plane killing everyone on board allows us to heal from the pain of that evil act, because we know that the reason those men committed such an evil act was in the form of self- interest. This is how 'collective karmic debt' is created, that takes years or lifetimes to erase. Could the current war between Russia and Ukraine, that started early in 2022, be karmic?

In the Bible we are told it takes up to seven generations for sins, bad karma, to be released and healed. Even the land around, where an evil act is committed, will hold negative karma within it that will be felt for many years.

This Earth and all life on it, plants, animals, birds, insects, sea creatures, must be perceived as sacred. The Lakota tribe in America have a special prayer, 'Mitakuye Oya sin Aho' to heal this Earth.

Swami Yatiswarananda (1889-1966) wrote - "The lines dividing the Self-mind, body, spirit, become more and more blurred, and finally the splendour of the Supreme Soul envelopes all existence." This is enlightenment, when we feel the world, and all life in it from the Soul.

'When my spirit grows faint within me, it is you Soul, who watch over my way.' Psalm 147 This verse was a favourite of St. Francis

Story of Saint Francis of Assisi.

Francis spent his young days having a good time. He was quite wild and in Assisi he was known as the "King of revelries' meaning someone who takes part in unrestrained merrymaking. His parents were very wealthy, so he did not have to work, and they allowed him to do whatever he wished.

One day Francis was walking past the ruins of an old church, that could not be used any more due to its dilapidated condition, when he heard a voice say to him, "Francesco fix my church." His first reaction was shock, at what the voice had told him, but then he decided to fix it, as a joke! The more he fixed the church the more he got interested in the renovations. He also discovered his finances were being quickly used up in fixing the old church and that there was not a lot left over for merry- making. But this did not bother him because he now had a purpose in his life, and he lost interest in doing what he did before.

This annoyed his friends immensely who still wanted his company, and his money, to keep up their social life.

One day while Francis was walking down a mountain path, singing to himself, his friends approached him from the opposite side and attacked him and then pushed him down a steep ravine that was filled with snow. After quite a struggle Francis crawled his way back to the top, bruised and bleeding from the beating they had given him. Francis put the experience behind him and restored the church back to its former glory, found a priest to hold services in it again, and later became a monk and was known as Friar Francis.

Years later one of the guys who had beaten him up came to the church and told the people what Francis had done to rebuild the church. Then he approached Francis privately and asked him if he forgave him. Francis said, "Oh that, all I remember is walking down the path singing."

From that experience Francis realized his purpose in life was to serve humanity. He said, 'We have been called to heal wounds, to unite what has fallen apart, and to bring home those who have lost their way.'

Francis knew he had a special connection to birds and animals. Once whilst travelling with some priests to Mount Verna they stopped to rest under a great oak tree and flocks of birds flew down and sat on his arms and shoulders.

After his death on the 3 October 1226, he appeared to some of the priests, whom he called brothers, and he told them he served the departed souls by leading them to God. He wrote the hymn, 'Make me a channel of your peace,' that is still sung today in Christian churches. Just saying these words or singing them can help us in our call to service.

Make Me A Channel of Your Peace

Make me a channel of your peace,
Where there is hatred, let me bring love.
Where there is injury, your pardon Lord,
And where there's doubt, true faith in you.
Make me a channel of your peace,
Where there is despair in life, let me bring hope,
Where there is darkness, only light.
And where there's sadness, only joy.
Master grant that I may never seek,
So much to be consoled as to console.
To be understood, as to understand
Or to be loved as to love with all my Soul.
Make me a channel of your peace,
It is in pardoning that we are pardoned,
It is in giving to all that we receive.
And in dying we are born to eternal life.

Saint Francis was so connected with Nature he saw God and Nature as one, the last song he wrote, Canticle of the Sun, was given to his fellow friars to sing daily.

'Praise my Lord through all His creatures, especially through my brother Sun, who gives Light and bears thy likeness.

Praise be to my Lord through Sister Moon and the Stars. In Heaven, you formed them clear and precious and beautiful.

Praise be to you my Lord through Mother Earth who sustains us, and governs us, and produces varied fruits with coloured flowers and herbs.

Praise be to you my Lord through our bodily death; from whom no living man can escape.

Blessed are those who do your will, for the second death shall do them no harm.

Praise and bless my Lord, and give Him thanks, and serve Him in great humility.'

Francesco Forgione, later known as Padre Pio, was born into a poor peasant family in 1860 in Pietrelcina in Southern Italy. Even before the age of 5 years he felt so connected to Saint Francis of Assisi he believed their souls were one, and at that very young age knew his destiny was to be a priest. At the age of 15 years, he entered the novitiate of the Capuchin friars at Morcone, and took vows of poverty, chastity, and obedience and travelled to the friary of Saint Francis of Assisi in Umbria. In that year, 1918, he received the permanent wounds on his hands and feet, the same wounds that Saint Francis received in 1224, known as stigmata; the wounds Jesus received on the cross at his crucifixion. His message to the people was to 'recognize God in all things.' In 1925 Padre Pio renovated an old convent into a medical clinic for those people in extreme need. Pio died in 1968 and later became Saint Padre Pio.

Holy men and women often return to Earth to help people towards enlightenment and samadhi, where there is no more karma, just the pure soul of illumination. This is the complete evolution of the mind to the Universal Mind, the Bodhisattva level of purity. In the Bible, John 10:30, Jesus says – "I and the Father are one. Believe the works themselves so that you may know and understand the father is in me and I AM in the father."

Music and singing can be healing for the soul and are a good way to distract the mind from negative thoughts.

When I was teaching in a school in the mainly Aboriginal town of Halls Creek in the far north of Western Australia, I had a little girl in my class, 7 years old who told me of an experience that would have left adults traumatized for a long time, yet she handled it extremely well. She had gone off camping in the bush, a day's journey from her home with her grandfather who after going hunting went back home and left her alone in the bush, he later said he had forgotten he had taken her. She was alone for a whole day and night. I asked her what she did during that time, as she must have been upset and confused. She said, "No miss I just singing, I am singing and singing, then my grandfather come back and took me home."

And recently four children from an Indigenous Colombian community were found alive five weeks after their plane crashed in thick jungle. Three adults, including the pilot died in the crash. The eldest child, a 13-year-old girl, would have used her Indigenous intuitive gifts along with her spirit teachers to keep herself and her siblings, aged 9, 4 and 11 months, safe. It is also highly probable that she drew on wisdom from past lifetimes to survive, and keep her siblings alive, in such a harsh environment for so long.

Along with singing, affirmations can restore good karma. This is a good one to say often:

I regret all the harm I have committed towards myself and others in the past.

From now on all my actions will be motivated by good-will towards myself and others.

May this affirmation connect me with the heart wisdom to be able to do so.

Fear is a crippling emotion and if it is not properly dealt with can sabotage every aspect of one's life until one has no confidence left to be of service to others. Remember it is only our good service that accumulates good karma for this life and the next.

I did a past-life regression on a young woman who had felt fearful all her life. At 49 years of age, she wanted to be free of fear and have courage to take some risks in life, because she felt she had missed out on some good opportunities in life due to her feelings of imagined fear. We decided to do a past-life regression to see if the fears she could not explain came from a past life experience.

In the past- life regression session she was a female, around 20 years old in 1840, she was quite sure about this date. She was wearing a skirt and blouse and a necklace of pearls and lace-up boots. On her head she wore a beret, and she was carrying a suitcase. She was standing at the train station with a lot of other people. The train pulled into the station, and she got into a carriage and sat down with her suitcase on her lap holding on to the leather strap. She felt excited.

The train was moving along quite fast, and she could 'hear' the sound of the wheels on the track. It was daylight. Then the train entered a tunnel, there was a loud screeching of brakes, rocks were blocking the tunnel, with the train smashing into the rocks. There was a lot of screaming coming from the passengers. People could not get out. She feels trapped. Then she sees a smashed window near her. She crawls out onto the track. A guy in a brown suit is calling out for help. Rocks are everywhere. She moves to the guy, there is a lot of blood on him, but she 'knows' he is going to be ok. The screaming for help is deafening. There is utter chaos around her.

After that 'fearful' past life experience her life changed. She embarked on a massive career change, left her current safe employment, and studied at university as a mature-age student, and is now a nurse at a large hospital, and loves her job of caring for others.

Fear stops us from going forward and learning new skills with the acquisition of new knowledge, that becomes accessible to us in our next life. Even our scariest memories can be healed through understanding the experience that created it. With this new awareness the memory becomes an experience, without the feeling of fear associated with it. Past-life therapy helps to remove fear from the memory field, that prevents us from taking risks, so we can move forward. EMDR, Eye Movement Desensitization Reprocessing, helps resolve upsetting memories. Recognized by the World Health Organization, it was developed by Francine Shapiro in 1982 to help people to heal from traumatic memories that are 'stuck in the brain.' What about memories 'stuck in the samskara?'

I did another regression where a young girl had convinced herself her relationships would not last because, she 'believed' her boyfriend would leave her. She went for positive training, did mindfulness but still could not shift this strong belief that the guy in her life would not stay with her long term. She finally put it down to being let down by a boy when she was a young teenager and had not been able to move on from that.

Then she did a past-life regression and a memory from a past life came to her like a black and white movie. 'She was young and happy eating dinner with her family. She was 17 and the love of her life was 20. His name was John. He was her soul mate, she felt it. They were planning their wedding, looking into the shops, cuddling, holding hands, and laughing. The warm feeling of love totally engulfed her as she stepped into a shop. John had gone across the street. She heard the screeching of car brakes, everyone ran out of the shop, and she went too. Someone had been hit by a car. There was a body lying on the street. She ran to it. It was John.

She cradled him in her arms, crying, telling him she loved him. Her last memory of that lifetime was sitting staring at his funeral casket.'

She felt a victim and stayed a victim in that past life, never allowing herself to find love again. Now in this lifetime she was afraid any boyfriend would leave her if the relationship got too serious.

After the regression she was able to let go of that past life experience and open herself to being in a loving relationship in this present life, that brought her the added joy of becoming a mother.

Many of the Indigenous people in Australia today have difficulty in letting go of the wrongs that were inflicted on their people in the past and will constantly re-call the stolen generation. The only way they can bring healing to those past experiences of pain and suffering is by letting go of the need to continually blame the people who inflicted that pain on their people over one hundred years ago. Hanging onto these negative memories has become collective bad karma for their whole community. Letting go of the past and creating new experiences of good service to others will bring good karma that will reward their whole community.

When we move forward, we still acknowledge the wrongs of the past, because that is our history (story), but it does not influence our future, because it is not our burden to carry anymore. Always bear in mind too that the possibility of the victims of today being the perpetrators of yesterday are highly possible. So, in truth blaming those pioneers of the past for their ill treatment of the Indigenous people could be blame towards oneself from a past life. Unless everyone knows exactly who they were in their past lives and what they did, you cannot blame anyone, because if you did you might have to point the finger at yourself and where do you go from there? You simply build up more bad karma because now you hate your past life character as much as the others.

Clearing bad karma from our Samskara seems like a never-ending painful affair but each painful experience we overcome with inner strength, that involves forgiveness, brings us closer to eliminating all bad karma from our samskara and allows us to work with the light energy. Our good karma, and the blessings they bring in each lifetime, can never be taken away from us. What is yours will never be withheld from you.

Here is a simple ceremony that can be done to heal generational curses, wrongdoings, that have been used by Shamanic Healers for thousands of years. It is a fire ceremony to heal our ancestorial curses so we can live harmoniously with all people. This ceremony should be done with a group of like-minded people where the belief in their own power to heal is strong.

Fire Ceremony – Sit in a circle around a small fire with family members, or other people who wish to release all negative family trauma, believing it is your karmic duty to break the cords of ancestral curses. Have in your hand as many sticks as you would like to represent each karmic pattern you need to destroy, burn. For example, you might wish to destroy generational scarcity, so that you and your family can have everything that you need in this lifetime. Or you might wish to stop the pattern of abuse that is in your family.

Blow on your stick and say, 'From this moment on my family is released from all generational scarcity." Throw your stick into the fire and watch it burn and disappear.

Use a different stick to release the next karmic curse, breathe on this second stick, speak out the next ancestral curse you want to destroy, "I release all abuse and violence from my family and home," and throw this second stick into the fire and watch it burn.

Keep doing this sacred ritual till you are free from all negative family karma, then move onto the next person until everyone in the circle has had their turn.

Finish off the ceremony by chanting together, 'Thank You, Thank You, Thank You,' to the Higher Powers for their gift of healing your generational curses.

People who have come to this lifetime with high levels of Sattva Guna have the 'Midas' touch, for them it is never a case of one step forward and two steps back, they just keep moving forward making the world a better place for themselves and others. On the other hand, those who are born with high levels of Tamas Guna, ignorance, gaining wisdom through knowledge and other people's good advice will be difficult for them. Yogis say that their wisdom will only come through their own suffering. My mother used to call it, 'learning the hard way.'

Some people say we need to have the bad experiences to appreciate the good ones. There is no truth in that because the bad experiences we have now is clearing negative karma from our samskara. We have already felt loss, cruelty, and suffering from our multiple past lives. If we did not have so much bad karma to clear from our samskara we could move forward faster, whereas negative, difficult experiences can block our energy so strongly we have to stop – sometimes for years – before we can re-gain our strength and confidence to carry on serving others in a healthy positive way. Because some bad experiences are so overwhelming, they can destroy that person's life through an early death or suicide. This hinders us from collecting good karma, therefore less Sattva Guna in the samskara for the next life.

Saint Francis was still young when he turned himself around from being someone who took into someone who gave. Unfortunately, some people only come to this awareness later in life, when their human body has become worn out and tired from the high cost of living a busy, often social, life. Neglecting to properly care for our body can result in the body breaking down sooner. This body we come with comes with no guarantee as to how long it is going to be able to hang around on Earth, it could break down at any time and the Soul will have to leave. A bit like the Nursery Rhyme Humpty Dumpty – "All the Kings horses and all the Kings men couldn't put Humpty together again."

It is important to clear bad karma in our present lifetime, so the younger we are when we start the better. Some people start off early in life collecting heaps of bad karma through their selfishness then have little time to clear the backlog of present and past bad karma. If having a 'good time' involved hurting others, then that lifetime was not a good time.

But the Soul will be back after it has re-united with the LIGHT for some time, even though time on the other side is different to our linear time here. Over here, for us humans, even a hundred years on Earth is merely moments over there in spiritual form.

Recently our newspapers were full of the story of a man who murdered three young women in our city, with many people writing into the newspaper expressing their thoughts and feelings. One woman's letter went like this; 'We don't know what twists the judgment of people who murder from starting life as innocent babies.'

Unfortunately, not many come here as innocent babies. People who have committed heinous crimes, like Hitler, do die and return. Unfortunately, few remember what they did or how they lived before this life, but the samskara has all the memories of each lifetime stored within it.

Dr. Ian Stevenson of the University of Virginia collected re-incarnation stories of children for many years because he found that their memory of their past life was still 'fresh' in their mind. Through thorough research he was able to back up these stories with reliable facts.

In Vietnam he met a young sergeant named Thiang San Kla who told Dr. Stevenson that he was his Uncle Ploh reborn. His parents, who were Buddhists and followed the belief in re-incarnation, also believed he was his Uncle Ploh re-born as their child from the birth marks he was born with – a large birthmark on the baby's body that was in the same place where the knife had pierced Ploh's body, that took his life. Uncle Ploh had been tattooed on both hands and feet, Thiang San Kla was born with tattoo-like markings on hands and feet, and Uncle Ploh had had a festering wound on his right big toe for years, when Thiang San Kla was born he had a deformed right big toe!

In India, in the state of Punjab, there lived a Sikh girl called Kamaljit Kaur. From the age of about three years, she kept asking her parents to take her home. They told her she was living in her home, and that this house was her home. But she kept saying, "This is not my home." When she was about 6 years old, she asked her father to take her to the village near the town of Ambala. Her father wondered how she knew about any village near Ambala. There had been no talk about that village in their home and neither he, nor his wife, knew about any village nearby. Nonetheless he made enquiries and found out the name of that village, and how to get there, so he could take Kamaljit there, as she had been asking him to do for some time. As they entered the village, she pointed out the courthouse, the little school she attended, and the local hospital where she said she had been treated for her injuries. Her father asked, "What injuries?" Kamaljit told him she had been hit by a bus whilst riding her bike home from school. She told him her injuries were so sever she had bled to death. She was able to direct her father to a small cluster of homes and picked out the one where she said she had lived, and said, "there is my house!" The family living in that house welcomed them in and Kamaljit's father explained why they had come. He said, "my daughter very much wanted to see you because she believes she lived in this family in her previous life." The family confirmed they had lost a child nearly ten years ago in a bad accident, and they had never gotten over their daughter's death. They brought out a class photo taken just before their daughter died and Kamaljit was able to name every student in that class photo accurately.

As her parents were not familiar with that village, or who lived there, Kamaljit had no way of knowing students in the local school from 10 years before. Also, she was able to re-count the accident she had with the bus in detail, even to the place where she died, all of which this family confirmed. She even remembered her name in that lifetime, Rishma, when no one had mentioned that name! The mother in that family showed them a new maroon shalwar kameez, pants and top outfit, they had bought for Rishma to wear but she never got to wear it, and for ten years she had kept it, still new. Kamaljit remembered the outfit and her father said that from the age of four she had only wanted his wife, her mother, to buy her a maroon shalwar kameez. This family was convinced, beyond any doubt, that Kamaljit was their Rishma, re-born into another family. Kamaljit would have chosen to return to her past life parents but perhaps they could not have, or did not want, any more children, so she came back to parents who lived nearby.

Jim Tucker, Professor of child psychiatry and neuro-behavioral studies at the University of Virginia in America received a letter from a mother in Oklahoma saying neither she nor her husband could understand why their 5-year-old son Ryan kept crying and asking to go to Hollywood. He told them he was an actor in his past life and that he had been a dancer and had even danced on Broadway. His stories of being an actor were constant. He said he had travelled on big boats and had seen the world, and in Hollywood he even had his own agency.

To make sense of all this his mother went to the library and brought home some old movie magazines. Whilst they were looking through them, they came across an old movie called 'Night after Night' and Ryan pointed out to two men in the picture, one he said was his friend George and the other actor was him. Ryan told his parents he lived in a big house with a swimming pool on Rock Street. He also told them he died in 1964 when he was 51 years old.

His mother sent all this information to Professor Jim Tucker who checked it out and discovered that the two men in the movie Night after Night were George Raft and Marty Martin. Professor Tucker also found out that Marty Martin had danced on Broadway in New York, he had travelled on the ship Queen Mary to Paris, he had lived in a big house with a swimming pool on North Rock Street and he had owned a successful talent agency in Hollywood. But his death certificate gave his age as 59 years. After further investigation Professor Tucker found out that Marty Martin had died in 1964 at 51 years, as Ryan had said, but it had been incorrectly recorded on his death certificate as 59 years.

5-year-old Ryan had accurately given fifty facts about Marty Martin that he would have had no way of knowing except through a past life memory as Marty Martin.

The popular board game of Snakes and Ladders was invented by a Hindu man to teach his children the process of death and re-birth. Going up the ladder was the completion of that life, with moving up to Heaven. Coming down the snake was the return to earth for yet another chance of life on it. The number of ladders and snakes on the board depicted the countless number of times of our re-birth till we eventually get it right and attain enlightenment. Getting home, with no more rebirths, was the winner of the game.

Aesop, a Greek storyteller from around 620BCE wrote stories called fables to teach and give children an understanding of good karma through living a giving and compassionate life.

One fable told a tale of a dog running home with a juicy bone in his mouth. On his way home he had to cross a bridge over a stream. As he was running over the bridge he looked down into the water and thought he saw another dog with a big juicy bone in his mouth looking at him. He thought "If I frighten that dog, he will drop his bone and then I can have two bones." So, he opened his mouth and growled loudly at the other dog, that was really his own reflection in the water, and in doing that the bone in his mouth dropped into the stream and he went home without a bone.

This little story explains what excessive Rajas Guna, greed, and desire, does in the end.

Another 'fable' he wrote was, "A hound who had been excellent in his time and had done good service to his master became worn out with the weight of years. One day when hunting he caught a wild boar, but his teeth gave way, and the boar escaped. His master severely scolded the hound for letting the boar get away. The old hound replied, "Remember what I was, rather than abuse me for what I am." Here then is a lesson in empathy and compassion, and gratitude for the many years of faithful service the dog gave his master when he was younger.

The belief of re-incarnation was with humankind from the beginning of human life on earth. All the ancient tribes believed in previous lives, along with the Egyptians, Romans, and Greeks, and belief in re-birth existed amongst Christians in the early history of Christianity. Origen one of the early Christian leaders wrote in 3AD 'Each soul comes to this world reinforced by the victories or enfeebled by the defects of its previous lives.'

Plotinus was a philosopher who travelled extensively in his quest for Truth. For Plotinus, the soul's proper duty was to enter the material realm (earth) to care for it and to experience life in all its fullness. He was the first to give us the idea of Earth as a school, where he said the soul learns its own nature – the true self.

Plotinus wrote a lengthy essay against the Christian church, criticizing them for seeing the world as an evil place. He said life was holy once it was seen from a spiritual point of view. He wrote that life was an 'enchantment' when seen under the light of sympathy, and the purpose for the embodied soul's return was for the cultivation of virtue. Plotinus said, 'Try to raise the Divine in yourselves to the Divine in all.' He lived at a time when Christianity was about to be made the official religion of the Roman Empire, so his teachings had a huge influence on the early Christians.

According to scholars of theology re-incarnation was a belief of the early Christian church. St. Augustine (c354-430) of the Christian faith grew up with his father's belief in the philosophies of Plotinus and incorporated them into the early church. And there is evidence that St. Paul also believed in the works of Plotinus.

In the New Testament Bible, Matthew 17:12, we find unmistakable reference to the belief of reincarnation. During the vision of the Transfiguration on the top of the mountain, the Apostles saw the figures of Moses and Elias on either side of Jesus. Elias (or Elijah) was an ancient Jewish prophet who had lived in Israel some 850 years before. Referring to the ancient prophet Elijah, Jesus said, "That Elias has come already," and his disciples understood that he was referring to John the Baptist, who was baptizing people in the river Jordon around the year 20A.D. Jesus considered John the Baptist as the reincarnation of Elias, Elijah. Reincarnation was also in the Jewish tradition and in Islam. So why was it not included in their sacred texts? Or was it misinterpreted intentionally? Or was it because early religious institutions needed to control their followers with fear, so God was depicted as one who should be feared. God was also portrayed as a vengeful male figure, "Vengeance is mine, saith the Lord." (Romans12: 19)

In all the sacred texts there is the story of God banishing his people from the Garden of Eden because they had eaten the fruit from the tree of knowledge. Why would God banish his own creation? And wouldn't God want his people to seek knowledge, which is Truth? In Proverbs 3:13 God says, "Blessed are those who find wisdom, those who gain understanding."

The belief in people being given more than one chance to make a wrong right would have diminished the image of a God who was vengeful; and the hierarchies of the Church would have had little or no control in getting the people to unquestioningly follow their teachings and the belief that, if they followed the guidance of their leaders, they would go to Heaven. Otherwise, it was hell, a terrible place where you burnt forever. Like in the Garden of Eden, you only got one chance.

The sixteenth century Reformation, led by Martin Luther in Germany, when almost 100,000 people were killed by the Roman Catholic Church for opposing some of their teachings, could be interpreted as another form of control over the people for not doing exactly as the church preached. Even karma, though not referred to by that word, was pardoned by a letter.

In 1517, Pope Leo had letters of Indulgence or pardon letters sold to the people so that when they died their 'Pardon' letter would release them from all wrongdoing in their life so they could go straight to Heaven. Martin Luther called the costly 'Letters of Pardon' a great fraud and told the people everyone could be forgiven with 'true repentance and a willingness to change their path.' He said he was willing to die for Christ and the Truth, and strongly discouraged the people from purchasing these 'fraud' letters of pardon from Pope Leo.

A relative of mine who practices the Catholic faith told me she did not like the word Karma as it was against her beliefs. For her the word retribution was the word Catholics used instead of karma. The meaning for retribution, as it is in the dictionary, is 'punishment or vengeance for evil deeds,' and excludes forgiveness. Karma, on the other hand, means 'a person's actions affecting his or her fate in this life or the next.' Karma can be negative or positive. Good karma brings blessings and rewards into our life whereas bad karma brings painful or difficult experiences into our life. The word karma covers all our experiences, good or bad.

In the Ramayana, one of the sacred texts of Hinduism, King Dasharatha, Rama's father, paid 'retribution' to a hermit couple who lived in the jungle, after he accidently shot their son, by building a temple where their son had been killed. Here the word 'retribution' is used as a form of payment for an unintentional wrong action; it was King Dasharatha's way of expressing his sincerest regrets for the grief he had caused the hermit couple.

God does not send us negative or positive experiences, it is only our karma, past and present, that stops us from experiencing eternal bliss. The plans we make for our life, and even those unplanned experiences that happen to us from 'out of the blue' are the result of karma from this life and previous lives.

Re-incarnation teaches free will, like the oak tree, the tree of freedom.

Swami Vivekananda said, "Every thought that we think, and every deed that we do, goes into the seed form and lives in the body in potential form, and after a time it emerges and bears its fruit. These 'fruits,' results, condition the life of man. He is not bound by any other laws, except those that he makes for himself."

The acorn holds the seed of the majestic oak tree, and this seed takes up to 18 months to mature and it contains the genetic data for the entire lifetime of the next oak tree. In a similar manner our samskara holds the blueprint of all our experiences on earth. Botanists cannot explain how oak trees are evolving to higher levels of gene flow, just as scientists cannot explain the evolution of the human mind to higher levels of consciousness. The person we are today, and how we live our lives, is a collection of all our many life experiences pieced together into a tapestry woven with experiences of love and hate; peace and war; joy and sorrow, rich and poor, black, and white, sickness and health and these experiences are in our infinite, formless Universal Mind.

Swami Umeshranand explained the evolution of the human mind; Our evolution begins in the Lower Mind, where our thoughts are conditioned by our survival, regardless of the cost to others or our planet. Over time our experiences take us into the Upper Mind, where we perceive control over others as the best for our chances to go forward. From here our senses and feelings evolve into the Higher Mind, where we connect to our creative abilities' music, art, literature, and the need to dominate and control is softened by the Higher Mind's aspirations. From here we move into the Over Mind, when we over think everything as we try to connect to what is real and what is false, or an illusion, and feel ourselves getting nearer to the Truth. From here the process of the evolution of the mind takes us into the Spiritual Mind, into our Soul consciousness, and we realize we are spiritual beings and work at bringing the body, mind, and soul into oneness. Yoga can bring about this spiritual alignment. From the Spiritual Mind we evolve into the Super Mind where we can manifest our thoughts, as the great sages and masters throughout the ages have done. The seventh level is the Cosmic Mind, this is when we have complete power over our own destiny, we are no longer attached to karma from past and present experiences. The highest level of our spiritual evolution is when our consciousness is one with the Universal Mind, when returning to this earth planet is our choice, as is also the length of time we wish to spend here. This is the I AM Supreme reality of the soul's evolution; the Bodhisattva, Angelic, level of purity has been attained. The final phase, Samadhi, the eighth limb of yoga, has been reached.

'Lord, lead me from untruth to truth; lead me from darkness to light; lead me from mortality to immortality.' Brihadaranyaka

People who have experienced dying, N.D.E. (near death experience) have a strong recollection of communicating through their mind while being on the other side, with a clear memory of their life experiences whilst in the earth realm. Raymond Moody who wrote 'Life After Life' the bestselling book that offers true experiences of those people declared clinically dead, had this to say after interviewing more than one hundred subjects who had experienced clinical death and been revived, "Many seemed to have returned with a new understanding of the world beyond, a vision which features not unilateral judgement, but rather cooperative development towards the ultimate end of self-realization. According to these new views, development of the Soul, especially in the spiritual faculties of love and knowledge, continues eternally."

Today those who research N.D.E. like Michael Newton, PH.D. who wrote Journey of Souls, say, 'Hypnotic Regression of a previous lifetime to the point of death reveals the same features as near-death and actual death experiences.'

Buddhists say re-incarnation means an ever-growing wealth of experience during each lifetime, when our journey through difficult and at times exhausting experiences will lead us to more insight, deeper feelings, richer talents and to having a greater understanding of ourselves and others, especially within our own families.

Have you ever wondered why families are so dysfunctional? No matter how hard you try you cannot make some relationships work? It is because the two of you share bad karma from a past life. Then in this lifetime feeling negative towards each other, that might lead to unkind behaviour, only increases the bad karma that is already there between the two of you. My mother said she had an 'ill-feeling' towards a family member, and later in my life I felt the same about a different family member. Sometimes I would feel drained of all my energy when we were in the same place together. Practicing detachment was difficult for me because we kept being drawn together due to family engagements. Then one day the answer came to me. I was in Wyoming at the beautiful Green River campground feeling one with all of nature when I thought of this relative. Instantly my body tensed up, the bliss was gone! So, I called upon my spirit guides to tell me why this animosity existed between us. Was it a past life memory that was causing this negativity between us? Instantly I felt a sharp pain at the base of my spine, it was as if the rock I was sitting on had lodged into my spine, then I was re-living a memory from another place and time.

'I was in Ontario; Canada and the year was 1786. My name was Pearl. I had a round face and a chubby short body. I was dressed in a plain dress, but I had a pretty apron tied around my waist, and my hair was done in a neat bun. I lived in a small town in a modest cottage. I never used the parlor, the front room, but I kept it fresh and clean. It had three nice chairs in it and a small table with flowers in a jar on it. There were two other rooms, a small bedroom, and the kitchen where I did my healings. One day a carriage stopped in front of my cottage and a tall 'handsome' woman, elegantly dressed came to see me. I opened the door before she could knock and took her into the parlor. I called her Ma'am. She said she wanted to fall pregnant, she said it matter-of-factly. It was clear she did not want to engage in any small talk with me. I told her she needed to be more relaxed and be interested in her husband and lovemaking. She was very rigid and said she had no time or interest in lovemaking, just interested in having a child. Producing a child seemed like some sort of obligation to her. I told her very politely that if she relaxed more and gave herself fully to enjoying creating a child it would happen. I gave her some nutmeg, then thanked her for coming, and she left.

Months passed and one day I got information that she was ridiculing me as a healer, even though she never told anyone that she had come to see me. She said it was what others had told her about me. Her husband was a prosperous merchant and the few people in the town worked for him in one way or another. People stopped coming to see me, days passed into weeks; I could no longer support myself and I felt completely isolated. I left. My last memory of that lifetime was getting into a coach with three boxes.'

I took a deep breath as I came back into full consciousness, and I knew instantly who that person was in this lifetime.

Memories do not change on their own. I now must see this person as someone who is also spiritually evolving so I can collect positive memories, in this lifetime, when we meet. Having a past life experience can liberate us from unconscious memories that distort our emotions, by giving us a new awareness of the situation that will allow compassion, instead of animosity, to be felt. To keep the chakra system open, especially the Svadisthana chakra, orange colour, we must be emotionally free from past life entanglements and judgements. Holding onto negative feelings about others, whether consciously or unconsciously, makes us bitter and stops us from having meaningful relationships.

Saying, 'I develop emotional self-mastery' often, helps us in the practice of detachment.

The choices we make in each lifetime is our responsibility and good or bad karma is the result of those choices, but do not let thoughts of the bad choices keep playing in your mind, each lifetime is to move forward, so replace the 'bad choice' thought with a 'best feeling' thought instead. This is the Choose Again method that allows us to go forward.

Al-Kindi (c801-873) a Muslim Arab and one of the greatest philosophers of his time, in his pursuit of Truth wrote that anyone could aspire to a higher level of consciousness, and achieve full perfection, and be liberated from being re-born. Or they could, after attaining liberation, choose to be reborn and return to this suffering world to guide others towards the light, when bliss of final peace is sacrificed to help others. Al-Kindi said true happiness is not dependent on external circumstances but is an inner accomplishment. He said bad karma came from desire and hatred, while good karma was attained through self-mastery of truth and generosity.

Henry Ford, the American philanthropist wrote, 'I adopted the theory of reincarnation when I was twenty-six. Religion offered nothing to the point. Even work could not give me complete satisfaction. Work is futile, if we cannot utilize the experience we collect in one life, in the next. When I discovered reincarnation time was no longer limited, I was no longer a slave to the hands of the clock. I would like to communicate to others the calmness that the long view of life gives to us.'

Cherish your present life and embrace the new life your death will bring. When we accept death as a valuable part of the evolution of our soul then only will we be able to fully live in the present.

From the Koran, the Holy book of the Muslims comes this verse, "How can you make denial of Allah, who made you live again when you died, will make you dead again, and then alive again, until you finally return to Him?" 2:28

NUMEROLOGY

Swami Umeshranand saw life and death in numbers. Our life he said is governed by numbers from the moment of birth until death. He said advanced souls can see life and death in numbers and all numbers had a karmic influence on us during our life on earth. Some numbers do help in bringing us good karma and other numbers can work against us.

The Hindu philosophy of numerology is called Yantra and is used to discover Gunas, traits, in someone's personality that they need to be aware off. Pythagoras said numbers had Souls as well as magical powers because the secrets locked within numbers are as infinite as the numbers themselves.

'Numbers are the Universal language offered by the Deity to humans as confirmation of the Truth.' (St. Augustine 354-430)

So how much time are we given to clear up bad karma and build up good karma?

An old popular saying was 'Who knows when their number is up?' and another was, 'Only the good die young,' meaning, the longer you are on earth, the more time one has, to clear up bad karma. The Chinese saw long life as a blessing for the same reason.

Some yogis believe we are each given a certain number of breaths for each life and death comes when we take the last one. There is a story in The Tibetan Book of Living and Dying that gives an example of this belief.

Khyentse Rinpoche was a young student at the monastery in Kham, Tibet when one day his Master and teacher told him his time had come to an end and that he was ready to die, but he asked Khyentse if that day, date, was a good day for his Soul to depart this lifetime. Khyentse checked the sacred scrolls and came back and told his Master the perfect day for him to succumb to death was on the Monday. The Master said, "Monday is three days away. Well, I think I can make it." Khyentse left him, but when he returned several hours later his Master was sitting in meditation but there was no sign of breathing, but a faint pulse was perceptible.

Khyentse sat quietly with his Master. Around midday his Master let out a loud exhale, opened his eyes and in a happy mood asked for lunch. This is Khyentse's story, 'He had been holding his breath for the whole of the morning session of meditation. The reason why he did this is that our lifespan is counted as a finite number of breaths, and the Master, knowing he was near the end of these, held his breath so that the final number would not be reached till the auspicious day. Just after lunch, the Master took a deep breath in, and held it until the evening. He did the same thing the next day, and the day after. When Monday came, he asked "Is today the auspicious day?" Yes, replied Khyentse. "Fine, I shall go today," said the Master. And that day, without any visible difficulty, the Master passed away in his meditation.'

Our mind is consumed by numbers from the moment of our birth - by the time, date, weight, length, of the new baby's body. And the completion of life on the death certificate is the time and date. So, our first recorded piece of paper and our last is a set of numbers.

Swami Umeshranand said we choose our date of birth, but only advanced souls can choose their time and date of death.

Ken's birth date was $1^{st}.3^{rd}$. (month), he died on the 11th of the 3rd month- date 11.3- and his time of death was 3.11 a.m. The full date of his death was 11.3.2020 which adds up to 9, the completion number in numerology, and the completion of Ken's present life.

Michael Collins was the pilot of the command module Apollo that took the first men to the moon. He married Patricia Finnegan on the 28 April 1957, and they were together for 57 years until her death in 2014. Michael said that he had been 'very, very, lucky' to have Patricia in his life. He chose the date of their wedding anniversary to join her again, he died on 28 April 2021, at the age of 90.

Understanding numerology will show us the connection numbers have on us that are linked to our past life experiences. Pythagoras saw numbers as archetypes to the secrets of the mind. St. Augustine said numbers lead us to the truth, and Thomas Brown the great botanist said the number 5 has a pattern that is found throughout nature. The Hindu Vedas say we need the vibration of numbers to further evolve towards higher states of consciousness in each lifetime. Our life is made up of numbers that tell the story of our journey. By becoming more aware of how numbers play out in our lives we can understand our experiences better.

In Numerology numbers go from 1 to 9, no matter how big a number is it is added down to a single digit, unless it is a karmic debt number like 13 that remains as 13, because it cannot be added down to 4. When this number appears in our life it is time to pay off karmic debt from previous lives. Some see it as a good thing, being given an opportunity to clear the slate of past sins, while others find dealing with so much chaos too traumatic.

When karmic debt number 13 comes into your life know you are clearing karmic debt from a past life and that is the reason for the bad experiences. When 13 shows up constantly in our everyday life there will be challenges to be met over some time. For instance, if you move into a house that is a number 13, or any numbers that add up to 13, you will be clearing karmic debt, this is a good thing because once this debt is cleared your consciousness will evolve towards enlightenment, but unfortunately the process of working with the energy of 13 can make many people fall apart with the stress and trauma of those challenges. Sometimes starting a new project on the 13th can result in disaster if karmic debt is being paid out simultaneously. Karmic debt is abuse of power from a previous lifetime. This number points to selfishness and a total disregard for others, it also means being cruel and irresponsible in a past life, so when 13 shows up it is giving us the opportunity to make a wrong right via our own suffering.

For good karma there are the Master numbers, 11, 22, and 33. When these numbers show up in your life it is reward time, so celebrate! These numbers give us even greater opportunities for doing good. With these numbers, 11, 22, 33, everything just falls into place, and it seems as if life is all too easy.

The number 8 represents Infinity and is a symbol for weaving life, death, and re- birth. It is the pathway into and out of life that connects us to the cosmos at the point where it joins, known as the knot. Some cultures connect 8 to the bee and the snake and see it as a luminous golden living current within the body that gets us in touch with the miraculous, to bring healing and wellness into our life. The serpents that twist up the staff of the caduceus, the symbol for medicine, make figure-of-eight shapes. This number is also associated with abundance and material wealth. Its karmic value is in learning the right use of material resources, and self-mastery over greed and desire, Rajas Guna. The lemniscate visualization brings benevolence and bliss into the conscious mind.

Close your eyes and imagine drawing figure 8 between both your eyes, crossing over at the 3rd. eye (the spot between your eyes) and allow yourself to go into a deep state of calmness.

Number 9 is the completion number and when this appears it is time to move on to better opportunities and experiences.

The zero in numerology encompasses everything yet stands for nothing. In Yantra it is the Cosmic egg, which like a seed represents potential and possibility as it is the building block for other numbers. Today, Research Scientist, Nassim Haramein says, 'The base of Quantum Physics is tied to Zero-Point Energy, an infinite amount of energy that we cannot ignore. This is the energy of Spacetime, the fundamental nature of our reality.' Adding on zeros to any number can make its value unlimited.

Even the letters in our name can be changed into a number when each letter is given its numerological meaning, whilst the missing numbers are an indication of what karmic lessons need to be worked on. The numbers added together that make up our name gives us our soul number. According to esoteric belief, we choose our name before birth, according to our karmic destiny and those experiences we need to have in each lifetime.

In the New Testament Bible, the Archangel Gabriel gave Mary the name Jesus to call her unborn son. The numbers in those letters gave Jesus the energy to complete his mission of service and sacrifice in that lifetime on earth. Some people change their name from what they were called at birth to address this imbalance of missing numbers, even though they do not consciously know this when they want to be called by another name, often saying they changed their name because they prefer the new name, but it is an unconscious karmic reason for doing so. If all the numbers, from 1 to 9, show up in a person's name it means that they have complete free will in this lifetime. They are not governed by karma, good or bad.

Two American Presidents were linked by numbers, both had 7 letters in their surname, by which they were addressed, and one served exactly

100 years before the other, making them connected by karma. Lincoln became President in 1860 and Kennedy in 1960.

And the connection becomes even more remarkable when you consider that Lincoln's secretary was named Kennedy, and Kennedy's secretary was named Lincoln. Lincoln's killer was John Wilkes Booth, whose names add up to 15; Kennedy's killer was Lee Harvey Oswald whose names also add up to 15.

Another interesting connection to numbers and American Presidents, all of them who were elected to office in a year ending with 0 were hit by an assassin's bullet, only Ronald Reagan survived the shot, the others all died. The numbers here suggest karmic connections between all these people.

Galileo the great Italian mathematician and physicist, died in 8.1.1642. Stephen Hawkins, also a physicist, said he was Galileo re-incarnated because he shared the same birthday, just 300 years later, on 8.1.1942.

Check how numbers interact in your life, and you too will see how vital they are in influencing the choices you make in this life.

Carl Jung said, 'we are born at a given moment, in a given place, and we have the qualities of the year and of the season in which we are born. From the beginning I had a sense of destiny as though my life was assigned to me by fate and had to be fulfilled. This gave me an inner security, and though I could never prove it to myself, it proved itself to me. I did not have this certainty, it had me.'

Interestingly the traditional deck of playing cards was used as a tool for divination with secret meanings and symbols behind the cards and is also used today in a game of solitaire to seek answers to life's problems. It is a game of concentration and is closely linked to numerology and our yearly calendar.

There are 52 weeks in a year and 52 cards in a deck; there are 13 cards in each suit and 13 weeks in each season; 4 suits in a deck of cards and 4 seasons in a year; 12 cards with faces on them and 12 months in a year. All the Court cards, Jacks, Queens, Kings, numbered as 11, 12 and 13 add up to 364 add 1 point for a Joker and they add up to the number of days in a year, 365, and some packs have 2 Jokers indicating the leap year. The cards help to focus the mind through concentration, Dharana, 'as a lamp in a sheltered spot does not flicker.' Bhagavad Gita

Numerologists believe numbers are the cosmic code of the Universe, and that numerology is a successful system for improving our current life, because it enables us to live in harmony with all of creation through its energy, thereby creating good karma.

Indian Vedic Astrology, Sidereal astrology, the celestial movements of the planets, is known as Jyotish, the Light of Intuition. This is a belief in Hinduism and was first only given to the initiated orally, as secret wisdom. It was to understand the Power of the Creator's energy and will for this planet. The initiated astrologers saw the rhythmic cycles of Earth according to the earth's proximity to the sun, the closer the earth and moon got to the sun, the more negative energy was created on earth; and during this time, they predicted the earth would experience more natural disasters, conflict, diseases, financial disruptions. When this happens, people have the choice to either collect good, or bad karma. Those who choose to live in a 'buddha verse,' rather than a negative- energy Universe, would develop more compassion, as their consciousness moved towards greater spiritual awareness. Their faith in themselves and the Divine source of all Creation will get stronger as they become more inclusive, and this will balance all their karma so they can attain moksha, the release from birth, death and re-birth. For others this disruptive time on Earth will increase their levels of fear, their ego will become stronger, as they assert their rights over others through deceptive means. The Christian Bible Psalms 46:5 "God is in the midst of her (Mother Earth), she shall not be moved; God shall help her."

Vedic Astrology is the doctrine of karma and re-incarnation, and according to how the stars and planets are aligned can predict how actions from past lives influence us in this life. The planets play an important role in our life and their energy is the driving force in shaping our destiny in each incarnation. Vedic astrology predicts our path through this lifetime, starting from the point of our time and place of birth. Each sign illuminates what lies within us, our fate, karma, for this lifetime. Understanding our birth chart can reveal many pre-ordained details of our future experiences connected to our relationships, career, health, wealth, etc.

We are born into the sign that will develop our personality the most, and we will live through all the signs until we master the positive attributes of them all.

Astrology provides our life plan and describes how the karmic seeds planted in our samskara will blossom over time. It uncovers when the events, experiences, foretold in our destiny will come to fruition. The planets take turns in each lifetime to become active in our life and we are influenced by their energy. Indian Rishis (great sages) based on their insight, wisdom, and observations connect individuals to the twelve zodiac signs according to the levels of the 3 Guna's that they have come with in this lifetime, and the level their soul has reached. Enlightened Souls come with little or no karma.

The birth of Jesus, a significant event for Christians makes a reference to Astrology in Matthew 2:2, The Magi asked, "Where is the one who has been born king of the Jews? We saw his star when it rose and have come to worship him."

At Christmas, people around the world sing the carol, 'Hark the herald Angels sing' and the words, 'born that man no more may die' refers to Jesus' birth releasing all from re-birth through enlightenment, the Christ Light.

Monology, the study of the different phases of the moon is also linked to our birth and past lives because each phase of the moon is an interpretation of the level of Guna's we are bringing with us when we are born. For example, a child born when the moon is at the waxing gibbous phase, the last stage before the moon reaches maximus illumination, are amazing mentors with good communication skills, a carry-on from a past life that can be used and taken further in this life. They will feel this energy each time the moon is waxing gibbously.

Utilizing the energy of the moon was a common way of life for thousands of years until the Christian church forbade it as a pagan ritual, to the extreme where people who used this energy to preform sacred ceremonies were ostracized or burnt at the stake!

Just as many people today follow astrology and read their star signs to help them better understand their life experiences, monology can be utilized in the same way by finding out what the moon looked like when you were born – moonglow.com – can help here, then check out how you feel when the moon is in this phase, do you have more energy and vitality? And according to monologists if you want to manifest your wishes make your intentions when there is a new moon, that 'bestowing of gifts period' lasts for a couple of nights. This is called the waning moon or the asking moon.

'Ask and ye shall receive,' said the Master Jesus. When the moon is at its fullest it is called the waxing moon. At this time fill your heart and mind with gratitude for all the blessings in your life, and this will bring more blessings your way. Standing outside and gazing at the moon gives us self-love, and this becomes true after you have done it a few times. The moon has a unique energy of light that makes you feel good about yourself and this manifests itself into self- love. It represents the emotional part of ourselves, and its energy can help us draw closer to people who are karmically right for us. By understanding the various Moon phrases and harnessing this lunar energy we can awaken a deeper consciousness, awareness, within us. When you look up at the full Moon imagine its light guiding you through this earthly journey and removing any darkness from this and previous lives.

Early Native Americans used the Moon when performing the sacred ceremony of We Tiko to remove the 'curse of evil,' usually when collective karma was causing disease and painful experiences within the tribe.

In Harriet Stowe's book Uncle Tom's Cabin, the little girl Topsy is asked, 'Do you know who made you?' "Nobody, as I knows on," says the child, "I spec I just grow'd."

Each lifetime we come here to spiritually 'grow' so our service to humanity can be done with unconditional kindness, or as Plotinus said, 'For the cultivation of Virtue.'

Romio Shrestha in his beautifully illustrated book, Celestial Gallery, says, 'When our minds are full of compassion, we are never alone; an infinite retinue of celestial beings accompanies us on our journey.' The Cosmos of Compassion pg.18

In the 1960's Christian missionaries at a Mission School reported seeing shining white beings in the African jungle. Then during the Jeunesse Rebellion in the Congo several hundred rebels, heavily armed, approached the school where 200 pupils and ten teachers lived. With only two guards to protect them the missionaries knew they did not have a chance of surviving, they would all be killed. But as the rebel soldiers advanced on the compound the missionaries suddenly saw them turn around and run away. The same thing happened on three successive days, and then they didn't return.

Sometime later one of the rebels was injured and brought to the hospital that was attached to the Mission School, for treatment. When he was asked why he and the other rebel soldiers had run away each time they had approached the school, he said they had seen the compound surrounded by an army of soldiers in white uniforms!

In this true story the missionaries used compassion in their service and did not bar the rebel soldier from receiving care in their hospital. Their gratitude to God and His Angels for saving them from the rebels must have been overwhelming.

'God will give His Angels charge of you, and on their hands, they will bear you up.' (Matthew 4:6)

Everything the Creator has given us here on earth is to sustain us on our earthly journey. The Sun gives life to all living creatures through the plants. The rain clouds give us the water we need, the energy from the Stars interacts with all life on Earth, and so it is with the Moon. Nothing is there by accident. The Law of Karma says the Soul has an Infinite past and an Infinite future to guide the destinies of individuals and society. When we tap into this wisdom, we can awaken our gifts from previous lifetimes.

Palmistry can also guide us on our life path. The lines and patterns on our hands are formed early in fetal life, during the twelfth week of gestation and they never change. The hands increase in size as the individual grows but the lines and patterns remain the same throughout life and are virtually indestructible – even ancient mummies have clear and identifiable handprints. No two people have the same pattern on their hands, this is even true with identical twins. Each person has a wholly original and unique set of skin markings that can be read and interpreted by palmists to identify personality and life experiences that are linked to past lives and karma.

Astrology, Numerology and Palmistry can give us important clues to our karma in this lifetime. They can point us to lessons we must learn in this life because we have not experienced, or addressed them, in past lives.

The use of gemstones to clear bad karma has been used in the sacred ritual of death and re-birth since the beginning of human life on earth. Crystals were used to heal and cleanse the Soul, because they emit energy on the electromagnetic waveband to cleanse the auric field, Samskara. Fuchsite is used after death because its energy has the power to release the Soul from the body after death so the Soul can travel on its own unique pathway; and the gemstone Obsidian is used in meditation to recall past life experiences to heal current life traumas, and it is placed near a person who is dying to absorb any negative energy from the environment.

Kunzite, a pink gemstone found in Myanmar, is believed to be an extremely spiritual stone. The high energy it emits protects the Samskara and strengthens it. This spiritual stone encourages humility and the willingness to serve. If you are just going to use one gemstone on your spiritual path, then this is the one for you.

Along with gemstones herbal oils are also used to vitalize the Soul of the dying person by raising their consciousness to a higher vibration into the spiritual zone. Before the crucifixion of Jesus one of his followers poured costly oil over Jesus' head and on his feet and Jesus said, "In pouring this oil on my body she has done it to prepare me for burial." Matthew 26:12

So, what happens after death?

Let us look at the Garuda Purana the sacred texts in Hinduism given by God Vishnu. The Garuda Puranas were composed in Sanskrit in the first millennium BCE and were about karma and re-birth; good versus evil, the practice of Sattva Guna, and the practice of puja (sacred ritual) and reverence to Shakti and Surya-namaskar, along with the theory of yoga where the goal is samadhi, enlightenment. Carvings relating to these ancient scripts from Garuda Purana can be seen at Delhi National Museum.

From the Garuda Purana: 'Death is a process: first there is disconnection of the earth sole chakras. About 4-5 hours before death the earth sole chakras situated below the feet gets detached, symbolizing disconnection from the earth plane. A few hours before a person dies their feet turn cold. When the actual time to depart arrives, Yama the god of death appears to guide the Soul.

Death severs the astral cord, which is the connection of the Soul to the body. Once this cord is cut the Soul becomes free of the body and moves up and out of the body.

If the Soul is attached to the body and refuses to leave, there is a slight movement of the face, hand, or leg after the person has died. This means that the Soul is unable to accept the body has died and it cannot be part of that body anymore. It wants the body to feel alive, so returns to that body. Since the astral cord has been broken the Soul cannot stay and is pushed upwards. There is a magnetic pull from above to go upwards. Now the Soul can hear many voices. These are the thoughts and words of any people in the room and the Soul now communicates with loved ones and can be heard at a higher frequency of sound waves. Unfortunately, most people cannot hear the Souls thoughts or feel them due to being weighed down by grief. By now the Soul is floating in the vicinity of our star chakra, (stretch both arms upwards and that is where the Soul will be,) seeing and hearing and feeling everything that is happening around. The Soul will move amongst loved ones connecting with them all in different ways and will stay until the body is cremated. Once the cremation of the body is completed the Soul is convinced that the main essence of its survival on earth is lost and the body it occupied for so many years has merged into the five elements. Now the Soul experiences complete freedom, the boundaries it had while being in the body are gone and it can travel anywhere by mere thought.

For seven days the Soul moves about its places of interest, perhaps its children and other loved ones. The Garuda Purana states that if a person loved their money in that previous lifetime, then the Soul will stay in the cupboard where their money is kept. If the Soul has severe tendencies to cling to some aspect of their past life, they can become earthbound and unable to leave. Sudden death, excessive grief from loved ones, guilt, can cause fear within the Soul that can block its energy from moving onto the astral plane. The Soul feels it needs a little more time to wait and finish before moving on. This keeps them hovering on the earth plane. But time is limited, and it is very, very, important that it crosses over within twelve days to the astral plane of existence, as the entry to the astral world closes to the Soul a few days after this. It then becomes an earthbound spirit and leads a very miserable existence as they are neither in their actual plane nor in a body to lead an earthly life. They may not be negative or harmful, but they are stuck and miserable. Hence healing and prayers are of utmost importance during this period so that the departed Soul crosses over to the designated astral plane peacefully. Prayers are vital, along with feelings of blessedness for the life of that Soul, to help it to cross over. The protection of the Soul to help it reach its destination in the astral world, is achieved through prayers. It is necessary that after the seven days the Soul moves further upwards to the periphery of the earth plane to cross over to the other side, where there is a big tunnel that the Soul goes through before it can reach the astral plane.

This is a crucial time for the Soul because if it is carrying any negative emotions of hatred, anger, or hurt it will deplete its energy to embrace the light. The Garuda Purana guides one to do many rituals to lessen the burdens of the Soul. All the rituals, prayers, and positive energy act like food for the Soul which will help it on its journey. At the end of the tunnel is a huge bright light signifying the entry into the astral realm.

In earth time this journey takes 11 days and then the Soul is reunited with its ancestors, including close friends, loved ones and relatives from past lives. The Soul will now connect with their spiritual Guide.

The Guide or Guides will take the Soul to the great Karmic Board where it will review its whole past life in the pure light. There is no God, no judge, the Soul will judge itself, like the way it judged others in that previous lifetime. It experiences guilt for all wrongdoings and asks for self-punishment to learn those lessons. Since the Soul is not bound by ego, judgement becomes the basis of the next lifetime. Based on this a complete life structure is created by the Soul, called the blueprint for the next life. All the incidents to be faced, all the future problems and challenges to be overcome are written in this new agreement for its next life. It is at this time that the Soul chooses, through free will, all the details of its next life, family, work, appearance, every detail it wants to feel and be in its next life, and the circumstances that will create them.'

The Garuda Purana gives this example: If someone killed his neighbour by smashing his head with a huge stone, he will ask for never-ending headaches in the next life so he can experience the pain his neighbour felt. This is how we will judge ourselves and in guilt ask for punishment. We must seek forgiveness and offer forgiveness. This decides the severity of punishment. The Garuda Purana says we must clear our emotions since the intensity of them creates our levels of karma. When we align with the higher frequencies of compassion, kindness, joy, and understanding we can change negative karma from the samskara. Our samskara is a map of our Souls' potential to the highest percentage of Sattva Guna. Then there is a cooling off period in that heavenly realm before the re-birth. It also depends on our urgency to evolve. We are reborn depending on what we asked for in the agreement. We choose our parents and enter the mother's womb either at the time of egg formation or during the 4th or 5th month of pregnancy, though sometimes the Soul can enter just before birth.

The time and place of birth constitutes our horoscope, which is the blueprint of this life. The stars and the dates and times just mirror the Souls agreement for its life on earth.

Once we are reborn, and for the next couple of months, the baby remembers its past life laughing and crying as it expresses itself.

The agreement starts now that we are once again completely on the earth plane and are quick to blame God and/or others for our difficult life! But we are just honouring our agreement. Whatever we have asked for and pre-decided is exactly what we receive.

We never die, we live on, death does not end anything, it is just a little break before we meet again.' Garuda Purana

Life comes from life. Matter has emerged from Life.

The Andean Sharman's also believe that we all originate from the Light, and we return to the light via this portal called Chakana.

The Last Goodbye (The creation hymn in Garuda Purana)
'Go forth, go forth upon those ancient pathways,
By which your former fathers have departed.
Thou shalt behold God Varuna, and Yama,
Both kings, in funeral offerings rejoicing.
Unite thou with the fathers and with Yama,
With Istapurta in the highest Heaven.
Leaving behind all blemish, homeward return,
United with thine own body, full of vigor.'

So according to the Garuda Purana we come here to fulfill our pre-ordained agreement using the Guna's as a guide to establish whether it is going to be a rough lifetime or an easy one.

The Hindu practice of cremation for their dead is symbolically linked to Alchemy. The flame of the fire is seen as the dance of joy, as Shiva, Lord of the dance, who brings the dance, or cycle of life, to an end in order that a new cycle of life may begin.

The fire purifies the Soul (Atman) and transforms the body into Air leaving only the ashes of the body behind, that belong to the Earth. Fire does not destroy, it simply transforms, like a smoking ceremony. The human body is changed from solid, into carbon dioxide, into the element of Air. The Soul is not destroyed but instead it is purified through Divine Alchemy, a process of earthly evolution from a lower level of consciousness to a higher level of re-birth, so that in the next life the samskara will contain a larger percentage of Sattva Guna, higher levels of moral and ethical codes of conduct, into a more spiritually evolved Being of love, and wisdom.

This Divine Alchemy can occur anytime during a person's life. It is Life and Light and it comes directly from the Godhead. It is Divine Energy, the Holy Spirit, the Kundalini.

In Christian belief it is called baptism by the Holy Spirit and is celebrated on The Day of Pentecost (Acts2:3-4) when Jesus' disciples were together in a house in Jerusalem – 'Suddenly a sound came like the rush of a mighty wind and there appeared to them tongues as of fire, distributed and resting on each one of them. And they were all filled with the Holy Spirit and began to speak in other tongues, as the Spirit gave them utterance.'

Divine Alchemy is a spiritual process that acts on all forms-superhuman, subhuman, animal, plant, and mineral. Every atom that exists emits the light of its fire as electrons in the atom, thus creating its own energy of fire. Each human soul is a unit of energy that stems from the Divine Creator, the higher your energy field resonates, the more aligned you are with the Holy Spirit and can see the Divine in everything. Then you're able to impact others with your own healing energy.

According to yogis the tissue which makes up the Vagus nerve, or 10th cranial nerve is the most receptive to this Divine Alchemy. This manifestation of spiritual fire also occurs via the chakras as the Kundalini energy. When this energy is aroused then only can a human soul reach enlightenment because an alchemical transmutation has occurred - alchemy has been performed with fire. 'My God is an all-consuming fire' Bible - Deuteronomy 9:3

Plotinus: Letter to Flaccus

'You ask, how can we know the Infinite? I answer, not by reason. It is the office of reason to distinguish and define. The Infinite, therefore, cannot be ranked among its objects. You can only apprehend the Infinite by a faculty superior to reason, by entering a state in which you are your finite self no longer – in which the Divine essence is communicated to you. This is ecstasy. It is the liberation of your mind from its finite consciousness. Like can only apprehend like; when you thus cease to be finite, you become one with the Infinite. In the reduction of your Soul to its simplest self, its Divine essence, you realize this union, this identity.'

In each lifetime we can still re-write our life story which is the gift of GRACE. The dictionary explains 'Grace' like this: - a delay or exemption granted for the payment of a debt. Christian's sing 'Amazing Grace' at funerals, part of the hymn goes like this:

'The Lord has promised good to me,

His word my hope secures.

He will my shield and portion be,

as long as life endures.

When we've been here ten thousand years,

bright shining as the sun.

We've no less days to sing God's praise,

Then when we first began.

Amazing Grace how sweet the sound,

That saved a wretch like me.

I once was lost but now am found.

Was blind, but now I see.'

The words, 'when we've been here ten thousand years' in this hymn does not mean that is how long we can hang around this earth in one lifetime, unlike the oak tree in Riverside County California that has been on this earth for 13,000 years, but is a reference to our many lifetimes here on earth, and the words, 'was blind but now I see' is the attaining of enlightenment at the end, which is, 'Amazing Grace.' And today U.S. researchers have found that singing the hymn Amazing Grace improves the blood flow to the heart!

According to esoteric belief everyone can change their karma when they use the light (energy) from within called Grace, or the gift of the Holy Spirit, and it is Grace that will lead us to the experiences we need at precisely the right time. John Newton who wrote Amazing Grace said the hymn was the fruit and expression of his own experiences. He was the captain of a slave ship that transported slaves from West Africa to America and was witness, and often a part of relentless cruelty to the kidnapped slaves. In fact, he referred to himself as the godless sailor! Whilst he was in the Royal Navy he met Mary Catlett, he was 17 years old and she was 14 but there was an instant connection between them, even though their personalities were vastly different- Mary was quiet and pious; but their friendship lasted through the years and in 1750 John married Mary and her quiet influence made him reconsider what he was doing to the innocent African people. Four years later, in 1754, he gave up the slave trade and he became an ardent abolitionist, and together he and Mary fought for England to end the trading of slaves. In 1779 he wrote Amazing Grace, that is sung all around the world today; at the time he said, "I am not the man I ought to be, I am not the man I wish to be, I am not the man I hope to be, but by the Grace of God, I am not the man I used to be."

Even though John Newton wrote the words for the hymn Amazing Grace, the composer of the melody is 'Unknown', but it is recognized as a West African sorrow chant believed to have come from the slaves on the ship. In those times the black keys on the piano were called the slave scale, and some say the Negros were only allowed to play the black keys!

When a person I worked with died she had requested the hymn 'Amazing Grace' to be sung at her funeral with the words, 'that saved a wretch like me' changed to 'that saved and strengthened me' because she was adamant, she had been a good person throughout her life; but this hymn could also include past life behaviour that could have been despicable in another lifetime given the word 'wretch' means despicable?

'It is Grace that brought you here and it is Grace that will deliver. I prefer the hen that looks up to the sky than an eagle that flies high but is always looking down; how high is not the question, but how intense is your longing for the sky. May you always be in Grace.' Sadhguru

We can remove negative karma from this life, and past lives, by developing a personality of calmness and compassion, even in the face of obstacles and hardships, so that we can inspire others to be better versions of themselves, by radiating this aura of graciousness from within.

When we fully embrace the 'we' instead of the 'me' our impatient nature of rudeness and inconsideration of other's feelings will change into thoughtfulness towards other people. Accepting what others do for us with

148

gratitude, instead of complaining, is the first step to cleansing bad karma. But to get to this enlightened place we need to work on ourselves through many lifetimes, especially with the feeling of gratitude. Feel grateful as a vibration in every cell of your body. Just thinking it makes the grateful outside of you – feeling the deepness, the joy, the humility of gratitude, comes from within.

Breathe deeply into the belly, with the bundhas on, and experience the vibration of gratitude at a cellular level in your body, for the air that you breathe. Consistency is what we are after, because the real you will need to be like this ALL the time!

All the great masters and teachers isolated themselves from the material world so they could experience that inner peace before embarking on their role of service to humankind. Jesus spent forty days in the wilderness, Mohammed went to the top of a mountain, and Buddha sat under a Bodhi tree for several months before attaining enlightenment, which is the cleansing of all karma.

We need to be omniverts, which is a mix of extrovert and introvert. We need to be part of sharing our gifts and talents with the wider community but also be able to spend time alone, nurturing the inner self.

Most of us live lives of stress, chaos, and negative experiences, that becomes hard to ignore and let go of. We carry the hurt and pain and stress within and then fall into the trap of hurting others along the way as a coping mechanism. When we re-act to situations rather than responding to them we lose the ability to respond gracefully, we re-act by attacking another in a mean, spiteful way thereby heaping more bad karma onto ourselves, when instead we should be attracting good karma for ourselves, it is a case of 'do unto others as you wish they should do unto you.' Remember our unintentional mean actions collect the same bad karma as our intentional mean actions when you cause another person to feel pain.

To live a 'quiet' lifestyle in a world of chaos we need to de-stress our body and mind and always be in control of our emotions. Most people act irrationally under times of stress.

Stress is caused by our emotions. In teenagers the part of the brain responsible for the emotions are fully developed, often hyper-active, yet that part of the brain responsible for controlling the emotions, the pre-frontal cortex, does not develop until the age of 25. This means that that part of the brain that regulates the flow of emotions has not yet kicked in. So, teenagers experience powerful, overwhelming emotions, without the coping ability of how to deal with them. This is when teenagers clock up, big time, a lot of bad karma, by hurting others. Whether the actions are intentional, or unintentional, if their words or actions inflict pain, they collect bad karma, so pay back will happen at some time. And this is one of the main reasons for suicide amongst teenagers. Feelings of being overwhelmed, distressed and a lack of the ability to conceptualize consequences can often bring about a tragic outcome. Adults, on the other hand can have control over their emotions via the pre-frontal cortex, but for some women it gets disrupted again after giving birth and during the menopause.

Here are three easy steps to take to collect good karma:

Think in terms of we instead of me.

Service, every small thing that you do for another counts.

Discard the ego by not taking things personally.

WHEN WE FEEL BLESSED, WE CANNOT FEEL STRESSED

Holding a grudge brings stress. Understanding the experience brings clarity and creates a new way to remember, because now the memory does not stress you out. We know that the stress hormone, Cortisol, weakens the body's immune system, so making more and more cells that are stressed causes destress that brings on depression.

My husband was working in a hospital when a woman was brought in in a very destressed state and all she kept saying was, "when does it end, when does the pain and suffering end." It comes to an end when we replace feeling stressed with feeling blessed, even in the worst situations, if homeless, maybe in that moment, it is not raining. There is a blessing in that.

From little things big things grow, think of the tiny seed in the acorn that grows into the majestic oak tree. The more we practice feeling blessed we will be given more experiences of blessings, and as the blessings grow so will our good deeds, germinating into good karma. These karmic seeds planted in our samskara will blossom over time, enabling us to serve even more. Our behaviour is reflected by how we are feeling within. Good behaviour brings good karma, and bad behaviour brings destructive karma.

Paulo Coelho in his book Secrets writes, 'The fruit produces seeds, which transform once again into plants, which again bloom with flowers, which attract the bees, which fertilize the plant and cause it to produce yet more fruit, and so on and so forth until the end of eternity. Autumn, a time to leave all that is old, the terrors of the past, and make way for the new.'

'What a wonderful thought it is that some of the best days of our lives haven't even happened yet.' Anne Frank

Jan Morris was born in the U.K. in 1926, a male child called James who from the age of four felt she had been born into the wrong body and should really be a girl, her silent prayer continuously was, "please God let me be a girl." As James she married a woman, and they raised 4 children. But she never felt herself as a man and felt depressed with indecision and anxiety and even considered suicide. She travelled the 'expensive, fruitless path of psychiatrists and sexologists,' but never felt any better. In the early 1970s, after her marriage broke up, she underwent surgery and re-named herself Jan Morris and in 1974 she wrote her memoirs, Conundrum, that became a best-seller. At the time she said, "I no longer feel isolated and unreal, I am beginning to know how I feel myself." She became an acclaimed author and was even a Booker Prize finalist in 1985. She and her ex-wife reunited and were buried together under a stone inscribed in both Welsh and English, "Here lie two friends, at the end of one life."

If things are not working in your life change things wherever you can, give yourself a new name and call yourself by this new name, and remember this new person is never stressed. Every time you feel the peace call yourself by this new name and say with your arms upwards, 'I reach for the Heavens,' then put your hands down, bow your head, and say, 'and bend to the earth.'

Do this simple practice of gratitude often, especially when there is a full moon in the night sky, as the full moon represents our 'fullness' of blessings.

Life often does not turn out the way one hoped it would, instead of feeling frustrated and annoyed about how things turned out consciously change your thinking and choice of words till they sound something like this – "I may not have gone where I intended to go; but I think I have ended up where I needed to be." This will help you to let go of any stress caused by feelings of disappointment.

Dr. Bruce Lipton a cell biologist from the University of Wisconsin's School of Medicine says in his book, The Biology of Belief, "We are not victims but masters of our fate."

What we tell ourselves, about ourselves, is what we come to believe about ourselves. Feeling 'inadequate' or 'not good enough' builds that belief within us, because it is in the samskara, and can last many lifetimes, unless we change it. We will see it when we believe it.

In olden times elephants were used to do a lot of the heavy carrying work in India, before trucks and other heavy transport was available. The owner of the elephants would train the elephant, whilst it was still a calf, by putting a rope around its leg and tying it to a post. At first the little elephant would tug and pull at the rope to try and break free, but no matter how hard he tried he stayed tied to that rope. Eventually the little elephant gave up. When the rope was tied to his leg, he knew he could not break free, thus it became an all- powerful, immovable force in the elephant's belief system. When it became fully grown just tying a rope around its leg, not even tied up to a post, would keep it immobile and docile.

When a false belief permeates our mind, we limit ourselves to fewer possibilities. We tell ourselves we could never achieve a certain goal, or lasting happiness, or even peacefulness in our life. We embrace doom and gloom more readily if that is what we believe life has for us.

What beliefs, programing, habits, stop you from expressing your true self? What is holding you back from serving others? What is stopping you from tuning into your higher self? Sometimes it could simply be because your mind is confined to reality as you have been taught to see it, and you believe there is no other way of it being a possibility. Remember these are just thoughts in the mind that refuse to change because they are so deep seated and even if you experience otherwise, you will hang onto the old belief because it feels more comfortable, in other words you are more used to the old ways, because the mind says you cannot change them. So, if there is a belief that you cannot manage your everyday life without alcohol, and someone gives you evidence that too much alcohol is bad for your health, you will not believe it, because you are more comfortable with the original belief you held in your mind that alcohol is ok.

It is the same with karma, if we hurt others, but believe we are not hurting them, we collect bad karma that will have to be paid back at some point.

Causing pain to another by our words or actions always brings back a bad re-action. Hurting life on this earth by our selfish desires will collect bad karma that will have to be paid back through our own suffering sooner or later, but karma will happen. After the Master Jesus died, he appeared to his disciples in spirit form, using his breath he blessed them and sent them on their way to serve all people. He also told the disciples they could forgive people's sins, but that not all sins could be forgiven. John 20:19-23

Here Jesus was referring to karmic sins, that had to be worked through by the individual, often through suffering, for the person to fully understand their wrongdoing.

Sadhguru, in his book Essential Wisdom, says that what is karmic can only be healed through the consciousness (energy) of that person. He gives the example of asthma that can be healed through kriya yoga, pranayama, diet, and exercise; but if it is karmic then it cannot be healed – 'For those where there is no change, there are very strong karmic reasons that are causing the disease.' pg.207

There are several things we can do to enhance our life of service and remove bad karma. Remember carrying baggage of negative karma around leaves us with no energy to do good. We also, in our quiet moments, suffer from guilt over the wrong things we have said or done to others, and this guilt inhibits us from 'walking the talk' because we think, due to our past experiences we are not good enough to offer help, or advice, or guidance. We can return to our true self at any time in our life because our innate goodness is always within, waiting to be retrieved, so we can live our authentic self – the highest perception of our Soul's Truth.

To regain our self- respect, we need to start with self- love, and this is about self-care. Self- care is when you unselfishly care about every aspect of yourself, it is not about I, me, myself, but about building confidence in your self-worth in the ability to help others. Remember that the person you are with forever is you, so this 'you' person needs to be loved and nurtured and forgiven for past mistakes, never to be repeated. This is not the new you, it is the real you. It is about self- acceptance not self- condemnation. Start by looking after your body, accepting the physical features, because after all you did have a choice in choosing this body when you decided to return to earth in this lifetime. Doing yoga is amazing in creating a healthy body, mind, and spirit. Choose a style and environment that suits you, not because someone else wants you to join them but because making decisions on how you feel will bring self-respect. Once you begin to trust your feelings you will be ready to fully commit to serving others. We are here for that purpose, the world needs YOU – that is how important your existence on earth is, and when you honour this belief, you will attain self-respect and self-love in your ability to serve others. How you serve is not important, the act of serving is enough. The service that you do is unique to you and no one else can do it just like you. Your 'spot' on earth cannot be filled by anyone else. Your energy is needed here, just as powerfully as any of the others, to do GOOD. It is the same for nature; each tree, plant, animal, insect, bird, flower, sea creatures including the stars and the sun, and the moon, serves its purpose at that time on earth.

Practice detachment, by this I mean do not allow yourself to stress over the small stuff, and do not obsess over everything that does not match up to your expectations. Moving forwards, even by little steps, is the way to go. My yoga teacher Emma always said, "When any more would be too much, and any less is not enough." Find the proper balance in your service to others and in your expectations of yourself and others and detach yourself from things that are embedded in your pride and ego. Ancient Greeks identified two parts in each person, their psyche, soul, and persona, self-image, where our pride and ego stem from. The Soul is the higher self, without limitations, whereas the persona, lower self, is full of limitations.

Move away from people whose behaviour does not conform to your level of goodness. Trying to change them is controlling, and this is not coming from your place of inner peace. Threatening, using force, or withdrawing, is negative behaviour, and it usually makes the other person more antagonistic towards you.

To maintain calmness in all situations, and thereby inspire others, focus on your breath, a calm, controlled breath will show in your body language.

With calm breathing, silently voice your intentions for the situation to end in a positive way. Call upon God, or the Angels, or your Guides, or loved ones in spirit, to assist in this situation. Imagine the person who is causing you distress with a light above their head, opening them up to their highest goodness. Remember this is your service to another, to bring out the best in them, no matter what the circumstances, you are here to transform negative behaviour and change bad karma into good karma. That service will help others to evolve to higher states of being, because each moment is bringing us closer to the end of our time here on earth, so we need to utilize that time in collecting good karma because every moment of our life is important. Withdrawing and doing nothing is also wasting precious time on this earth, unless it is undertaken as a means for us to rejuvenate our spiritual nature. But even this must not become an indulgence of selfishness. Each moment is a moment of blessed growth and healing for ourselves, and others, because we all need to evolve to higher states of self-realization in each lifetime.

After any experience of conflict, the benefits of moving on from it are most important. So many people continue to let the experience bother them way after the event, they find it hard to let go and move on. Be sure to revel in your achievements and not just worry about your next challenge.

In the end what matters most is:

How well did you love?

How well did you live?

How well did you learn to let go.

Light a candle and feel an inner glow come over you and say,

"As I light this candle my true path shines before me. I believe everything is possible, the world lights up as I allow my inner light to shine. I never give up."

Here is a true story of faith and ingenuity – Over three hundred years ago the Burmese (Myanmar) army invaded Siam (Thailand), robbing and destroying everything on their path of war. When the Buddhist monks, living in a nearby temple, heard this they quickly covered up a golden statue of Buddha with clay. When the soldiers arrived at the Temple, they ignored the clay statue but killed the monks and all the people in the neighboring village. Years went bye and by this time the statue was believed to be made of clay by all who lived there, until, one day the monks tried to move it and a large chunk of clay fell off to reveal shining gold! Wisdom and strength can come to us in our darkest moments when we go within.

Use the image of an elephant in your mind and 'see' the image as strength with humility. Now imagine riding on the elephant's back and feel the rhythm of its body with the earth, feeling connected to the elephant, and the earth, and the sky. Let your energy mingle with all and feel powerful. You can do this visualization for someone else who might be feeling powerless due to trauma of some kind. Keep visualizing this person on the elephant until you 'feel' their power returning.

When we serve with the highest intentions of wanting good for someone else, we are serving another and that is our purpose for being here. Everyone can serve through their prayers and thoughts.

Here is a visualization you can do to help a stranger, whilst sitting in the comfort of your own home.

Start by placing 3 fingers on your 3rd. eye (the spot between your eyebrows) and feel a subtle movement of energy in that area. Yogis say when the 3rd eye is open, we are slow to judge, and quick to forgive.

Sit in meditation for a few minutes just focusing on your breath.

When a peaceful calmness flows through your body imagine you are driving in your car. You approach two large gates that are closed, there is a high wall around these gates. Park your car near the gates and get out. Lock your car and walk to the gates, see them opening and walk through them up a brick pathway to a large building and knock on the door. When it opens step inside and follow the corridor to the door at the end.

You are now in a large, brightly lit room. Go and sit on one of the chairs opposite the door. Many prisoners come into the room all dressed in the same prison clothes. Sit there feeling safe, and totally relaxed, looking down. Feel everyone leaving. Now feel someone sitting near you. Let the silence connect both of you. Reach out your hand, and feel a warm hand hold it. Let your light and healing energy flow through your head, heart, and hand into this person's hand. Not a word is said. Feel the hand releasing yours, and see the legs stand up and walk away.

Say silently, "In gratitude I accept God's complete forgiveness for both of us."

Now stand up and quietly leave this room. Walk down the corridor and through the front door. Down the brick pathway, through the large gates and get into your car and drive home. Your work of service is done.

The world is full of prisons. I do not know where in the world you went, but in that moment, you connected with a prisoner and let them know, telepathically, that you cared. Service comes in many forms so feel free to 'visit' a prison anytime to show a prisoner you care.

Karma means action but it is an action that influences your future, because whatever you do will come back to you whether in this life or the next. Karma includes thoughts and words as well as actions and is meant to make a person responsible for their own life and how they treat other people. Here is a true story of karma in action.

When Roger Lausier was four years old, he went on a holiday with his family to a beachside cottage. Whilst his parents were busy, he took off to the beach and walked into the water and disappeared under! Alice Blaise saw the child go into the water with no adult around and quickly jumped into the water and got him out and took him to his parents.

Many years later, when Roger was an adult, he visited the same beach and saw an older man struggling in the water. He quickly jumped in and brought the man back to shore. The man he saved was Alice's husband.

If we are willing to serve, the Universe will bring us countless opportunities to increase our levels of Sattva Guna.

Start with your own transformation towards a more caring and compassionate nature. A wonderful way to do this is to go outside at night and star-gaze. If it is cold, rug up and even take a hot-water bottle with you and look at the stars.

Gaze up at those stars like tiny fairy lights in the night sky, until there is a feeling of just you and the stars. Nothing else exists. Now feel a part of the vast Universe and feel connected. The world needs YOU.

Do this night after night, weather permitting, till healing happens for you. You will be surprised how soon the transformation occurs, and the dark night of the soul, becomes the starry glimmer of hope.

This is the time to grab onto anything that allows you to feel positive and enlarge it, blow it up bigger and bigger, use your imagination until you feel alive in this beautiful emotion of being positive about how special your life is here on earth, and how much others need you.

Little children love the nursery rhyme, 'Twinkle, twinkle little star, how I wonder what you are? Up above the world so high, like a diamond in the sky. Twinkle, twinkle little star, how I wonder what you are?'

You can sing it to feel that childhood joy and wonder again, or to release any trauma from your childhood.

Star gazing dissolves those negative thoughts when you contemplate the cosmos, you naturally feel special and protected. There is nothing to do but stop, watch, and reflect. And that is something that has numerous benefits for your mental, physical, and spiritual health. This can also help to release old patterns and fears from a previous life because our strongest memories bring us back to similar patterns, until we release them and have no fear of them.

Throughout the ages people on Earth have used symbols to protect them from negative energies, even negative thoughts, and feelings. Symbols can give people hope, and an inner feeling of calmness. Many symbols are regarded as sacred because they can attract power from the higher realms.

J.C. Cooper in his book, Traditional Symbols, writes 'The symbol goes beyond the individual to the Universal and is innate in the life of the spirit. It is the external expression of the higher Truth.'

One such symbol is the Ankh, or Looped Cross, or Cross of Life. It represents all life – Past, Present and Future and is dated to ancient Egypt. The Egyptians believed that the Afterlife was as meaningful as the present one. Later the Ankh was used by the Coptic Christians to reinforce Christ's message that there is life after death and appears in the Gospel of Judas (3A.D.) Today it is used by many people to gain more knowledge about the mysteries of life and is a powerful symbol in past-life regression work in clearing negative karma from the Samskara because it symbolizes the eternal Soul. If you purchase an Ankh, use these words when you hold it – 'Cross of Life, Cross of Light; protect me through the darkest night.' Meditating on this symbol brings Divine healing energy to oneself.

Song of the Ankh

I AM all that has ever been,
I AM all that is,
I AM all that ever shall be.

You can use the symbol of the Cross, and say these words, to remove negative thoughts from the mind.

The Cross

A symbol of hope when things go wrong.
A symbol of faith, to carry on.
A symbol of light, to show us the way.
A symbol of love, to use every day.
Jesus Christ is the same yesterday and today and forever – Hebrews 13:8

Use the sacred symbol of the OM to experience-
The Sound within every sound.
The Strength within our weakness.
The Peace within the chaos.
Shanti, Shanti, Shanti OM.
"In the beginning was the Word, and the Word was with God, and the Word was God." From the Gospel according to St. John, chapter 1 verse 1.

And in your day-to-day life, eat mindfully, be grateful for the food that the earth gives us, so we can give back our energy in service. Remember our purpose for being here is to serve.

Bless your food by saying, "I bless this gift of food that the earth has provided to nourish my body."

Bless the water too that you drink using this simple Divine activation process and feel a complete sense of blessedness in every cell in your body as you drink it. You can bless a large jug of water so you can drink it as healing water for a week. This Divine activation is simple to follow and is an ancient Hebrew incantation.

We can activate the healing properties in the water we drink to a higher level of purity by blessing it. Many scientists believe that water has some form of memory. These images were taken at the laboratory for water microphotography in Braun, Switzerland

The photo on the left is water taken straight out of the tap. The water on the right was taken from the same tap, but after being blessed showed a different pattern within the water, more crystals or sparkles appeared after the healing activation.

Place your hands on the sides of the bottle or jug of water.

Say aloud - Kadosh, Kadosh, Kadosh

Adonai Sebayoth

Holy, Holy, Holy,

Is the Lord God of Hosts. (Say it 3 x)

6-6-6; 9-9-9; 12-12-12

Blessed Beings of Light, come forth now, and project into this Sacred Healing Water, through my head, heart, and hands the most intensified activity of healing and transfiguration allowed on earth at this moment by cosmic law.

Charge, Charge, Charge every molecule of this sacred healing water with the Divine blueprint of Heaven on earth.

Charge, Charge, Charge every molecule of this sacred healing water with the immaculate concept of my physical, etheric, mental, and emotional bodies.

Charge, Charge, Charge every molecule of this sacred healing water with the truth of limitless physical perfection.

Charge, Charge, Charge, every molecule of this sacred healing water with God's limitless flow of abundance, transfiguring Divine love, eternal peace, and every other quality of God's perfection.

Seal this Divine Light in every electron of this sacred healing water.

I accept that this Divine Activation has been accomplished with God's full power.

It is done, and so it is.

Beloved I AM

Drinking this blessed water and eating your blessed food will cleanse your body, mind, and soul so you can offer your service with a pure heart.

Psalms 138:1 "I will praise thee with my whole heart."

In the book of Psalms 90:17 "May the gracious favour of God be upon us and prosper the work of our hands – O prosper the work of our hands."

In the Old Testament book of the Proverbs Solomon, the King of Israel, asks God to give women 'the fruit of her hands' because she, 'stretches out her hand to the poor and she reaches forth her hands to the needy.' Proverbs 31:20

The 'fruit of her hands' are just rewards, good karma, for good service.

Doing regular meditation, with the intention to never harm others, but to always seek their highest good will increase your levels of Sattva Guna. Even if you face difficult times your inner strength will always shine through, and you will 'jump' the hurdles quite effortlessly. Swami Satyananda who had a yoga school in Rishikesh, India said, "Tranquillizing the mind, if conscientiously followed, is sufficient to bestow upon its practitioner an unimaginable peace, that peace which passes all mundane understanding."

Sri Aurobindo said that through meditation one could acquire a new consciousness, the Truth consciousness, and be liberated from feelings that cause suffering, liberated from ignorance, liberated from desire, and liberated from the law of cause and effect, into complete self-mastery. He said trees and plants needed light from the sun to grow, but we can receive light from within when we meditate, and this helps us to grow spiritually.

Look at this black spot, for as long as you can, to clear all thoughts from your mind. Keep looking at it, giving it your full focus. Now close your eyes and open your mind to whatever you 'see.'

Look at the black spot again, giving it your full focus. Think of nothing else. There is just you and the black spot. Gaze at the spot for as long as you can. Now close your eyes, and again open your mind to whatever you 'see.'

Do this a few times until you feel your mind has reached a level of clear thinking.

This is the unblemished mind of clarity that allows you to embrace a higher level of pure consciousness.

Sometimes people come into our lives and no matter how much we try to love and care for them they sometimes see our kind heartedness as a sign of weakness and can sometimes abuse our act of goodness by hurting us quite harshly. When you are the innocent victim of their abuse you can stop that person from continuing the abuse of yourself, and others, by performing this ritual called Kala Puja.

Before performing this sacred ritual, Kala Puja, one must be 100% sure it is for that person's karmic, and spiritual, benefit. This ritual will inflict some form of crisis in the offender's life; they will in some way be blocked from doing more harm.

There must be nothing in it for you, no revenge or self-satisfaction. Otherwise, this action might turn around and harm you instead.

Only use it when all other avenues of guidance have failed and never, never have any thoughts of what type of crisis you would like to see inflicted upon that person.

The type of crisis they experience must be left entirely in the Divine's hands. God knows best, so do not tamper with it. The Holy Bible, Romans12:19 says, 'Justice is mine, says the Lord." So, once you have done the puja let it go with thanksgiving.

All the chakras must be unblocked, use the words and intentions I gave earlier in this book (page 102), and one must be very grounded, you must not be holding onto any negative issues yourself if you want to perform this type of karmic release.

There is reference of this kind of karmic intervention by Saint Peter in the Christian faith, a bit harsh but nonetheless it certainly stopped the perpetrators from collecting any more bad karma in that lifetime when Peter's intervention brought death to the two people involved.

Acts 5: 5-10 'Peter said, Ananias why hath Satan filled thine heart, thou hast not lied unto men, but unto God. And Ananias hearing these words fell and gave up the ghost; and the young men carried him out and buried him.' Saint Peter also called Ananias' wife to be questioned about why she and her husband had conspired to steal from them after making a solemn commitment to God and the early Christian community, and, even after Peter gave her a second chance to confess, she stubbornly held onto her original story of lies. She too was condemned by Peter, and died instantly, and was buried alongside her husband.

The ancient Israelites had a cleansing ritual for people's sins that is recorded in the Old Testament in the Bible. Leviticus 14: 15-18

'The priest shall take some oil of the trespass offering and pour it into the palm of his left hand and dip his right finger in the oil and sprinkle the oil 7 times before the Lord. Then he shall put oil upon the tip of the right ear, that is to be cleansed and upon the thumb of his right hand, and upon the great toe of his right foot. And the remnant of the oil that is in the priest's hand he shall pour upon the head of him that is to be cleansed. And the priest shall make an atonement for him before the Lord.'

And here is a more recent story of a Jewish Rabbi performing Kala Puja.

A radical rabbi settler opposed to Israel's withdrawal from the Gaza Strip told Israeli television he was ready to hold a mystical Jewish ceremony, called a Pulsa Denura, to cast a death curse on Prime Minister Ariel Sharon.

Rabbi Yusef Dayan had held such a ceremony before the assassination of another Prime Minister Yitzhak Rabin in 1995.

Amongst the tribal Australian Aborigines, a similar ceremony called the 'pointing of the bone' was done to stop bad karma from hurting others.

These practices have been carried out throughout history, but when undertaken with compassion to help the wrongdoer in not creating bad karma for his/her next lifetime, it is an act of kindness and healing. It is not a quest for vengeance but to bring forth the Truth. The one thing we are certain of is karma will have to be paid back, so before it escalates into huge unsurmountable proportions its best to nip it in the bud through Kala Puja.

The Goddess of Mercy, Kwan Yin, gave humankind this beautiful prayer for cleansing one's soul, that can be said before performing Kala Puja.

May the health of God be in my body.
May the wisdom of God be in my mind.
May the light of God be in my soul.

May the purity of God be in my feelings.

May the grace of God be in my humility.

Kala Puja

A sacred ritual to stop or remove negative energy (karma) from absorbing into the samskara – subtle body.

Kala – black, negative, destructive, hateful, or evil.

Puja – sacred ritual.

This ritual is performed to stop someone's negative energy via their behaviour-

From harming themselves,

From harming yourself or others,

From harming the environment.

This is an act of spiritual kindness because it stops bad karma from building up, that might take many lifetimes to erase.

Before performing this ritual one must be 100% sure it is for that person's spiritual benefit, there must be nothing in it for you, no revenge or self-satisfaction.

All your chakras must be unblocked, and one must be grounded to perform this sacred ritual of karmic release.

Allow yourself 1 hour of uninterrupted time to do this.

Light candles, burn incense, and place some flowers in a bowl of water. Hold something symbolic in your hands like a cross, or mala beads, or a rosary, or a special gemstone that brings about healing.

Have inspirational music ready to play at the end.

Visualize the person who is creating the harm, and say this prayer:

Divine energy, protect me from my adversary.

Divine energy, shield me from all harm.

Divine energy, encompass me with your all- embracing light.

Chant – "Om Mani Padme Hum" for as long as you can. (This mantra removes negative karma from oneself and others and develops compassion)

Turn on the music and feel an enormous peace filling your heart and mind, and allow yourself to go into that quiet, quiet, place of deep meditation.

At the end of the meditation chant the Om and ring a bell with humble gratitude and visualize an elephant trumpeting.

For people with a Christian background, who wish to do this sacred ritual, follow the guidelines then substitute the prayer for Psalm 71: 1-6:

'To you Lord have I come for shelter,

Let me never be put to shame.

In your righteousness rescue and deliver me,

Incline your ear to me and save me.

Be for me a rock of refuge, a fortress to defend me.

For you are my rock and my stronghold.

Rescue me, O my God, from the hand of the wicked.

From the grasp of the pitiless and unjust.

For you Lord are my hope.

You are my confidence, O God, from my youth upward.

On you have I leaned since my birth.

You brought me out of my mother's womb,

And my praise is of you continually.'

Or you can choose this verse from Psalm 142:

'I cry aloud to the Lord,

I lift my voice to the Lord for mercy.

I pour out before God my complaint.

Before God I tell my trouble.

When my spirit grows faint within me.

It is You who watch over my way.'

Now say this prayer:

Lord, vindicate me against my adversary.

Lord, protect me from all harm.

Lord, shield me with the light of Christ. (Luke:18,3)

Chant:

Lord, have mercy, Christ have mercy, Lord, have mercy.

Glory to God in the highest and peace to ALL people on earth.

Do the meditation and at the end sing Amen 3x and gaze at a picture of the sacred heart of Jesus.

Helping others to do good instead of harm is the greatest service of all because they are being given an opportunity to transform their lives for the better. Swami Yatiswarananda (1889-1966) said the journey from doing evil to doing good was often a long and slow process, but we were never to give up in helping others to return to the light. He said, "The lines dividing the self, mind/body and the world we live in, and God, becomes more and more blurred, till finally the splendour of the supreme Soul envelopes all existence."

When we calm the mind through meditation and open our heart to love, gratitude, and compassion, we transcend the ego and are ready to live our Truth. This is when we connect with our soul, the I AM consciousness. This is the Blessedness of the Soul when we see the blessings in our life in all situations. It is transcending the lower level of consciousness to the higher levels of Soul power, when we count our blessings everyday of our life whilst here on earth. This is the abundance consciousness; the I AM consciousness.

Our purpose here, our service, is an exchange of energy that we use to give and receive. And when our time here is completed, our energy does not die, it simply changes form. Then our service continues from the other side. Our loved ones on the other side still support and help us in our life here on earth. Their guidance is spiritual rather than physical, though we can also be helped physically by loved ones and Angels from above.

I believe my mother served me from the other side when my house was robbed. Whilst I was out one day two men broke into my home and went through every cupboard and drawer in my house looking for money and expensive items to steal. I have 60 drawers all over my house, they opened 59, and threw the contents onto the floor. One drawer remained shut, the one with my gold bangles and jewelry in it. The amazing thing is the robbers opened the drawer above it and the drawer below it but did not open the middle one. Some of that jewelry was given to me by my mother. I believe she protected that drawer so they could not steal my precious pieces of jewelry. How she did it I do not know? All I know is that my gratitude was overwhelming.

Swami Umeshranand said, "We hardly know anything at all in comparison with what there is to know."

Our wisdom and strength come to us from a compassionate heart. Do this simple practice to develop a compassionate heart.

Press your thumbs to each fingertip and say Saa, Taa, Naa, Maa, 3x loudly, 3x softly, and 3x silently.

When we bring our hands together in prayer we connect with the cosmos, bringing the energy that is around us, and within us, together.

Our thumbs connect us to the element of Fire through the energy of the sun, and to our heart from where the passion arises. They also give us patience and strength to hang in there when life gets tough.

The index fingers connect us to the energy of Air, the 'Breath of Life.' They connect us to the lungs via the air we breathe and gives us the power to overcome depression.

The middle fingers hold the element of Ether, the energy that comes from the upper regions of the atmosphere, prana, that connects us to the Universal Mind, and dissolves anger. These fingers bring healing to the Nervous System.

Our ring fingers connect us to the Earth through our stomach. It grounds us to the Earth and releases worry.

The little fingers connect us to the element of Water and when we bring these two fingers together a subtle healing of the kidneys occurs. These fingers remove fear from the body.

Holding our hands together in prayer position brings about a deeper feeling of humility, where our needs become less, and our desire to serve becomes more. Namaste.

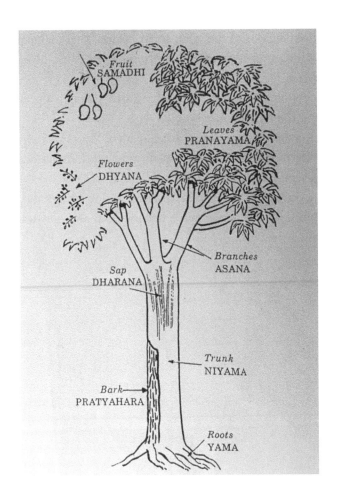

THE EIGHT LIMBS OF YOGA

'We're all going on an expotition with Christopher Robin and we're going to discover a Pole or something,' said Pooh to Piglet. 'Anyhow we're going to discover it.' A.A. Milne

Yoga is not merely the practice of asanas or poses, but the yoking together of the body, mind, and spirit, to achieve self-realization. The 'I AM' of the true self.

Shri Ramana Maharishi said, "Only try to know who you are. That is enough."

And this from Georg Feuerstein 'The Self is not to be found in the outside world but in the nucleus of our inmost being.'

The door to happiness opens from the inside. Buddha said, "Gain and loss, pleasure, and sorrow, come and go like the wind. To be happy rest like a giant tree amid them all."

Shamans say that the Tree of Life is the portal through which our Soul connects to the Universal Soul and this connection is enhanced when we practice the 8 Limbs of Yoga.

'Its roots connect us with the lower world, that of our conscious mind and our past.

The trunk connects us with the middle world, our conscious mind, and our life as it is now.

The branches connect us with the upper world, our higher consciousness that belongs to our future.'

When we practice the 8 Limbs of Yoga, we discover our true Self. Simply practicing the poses is not the true purpose of yoga, because it is just one part of what yoga is all about.

Patanjali interpreted the 8 Limbs of Yoga as the 8-fold path to enlightenment. A true yogi is called to undertake all 8 paths to heal their body, mind, and soul, so everyone can reach their highest potential in each lifetime. It is designed to dissolve rajas and tamas guna from the samskara so one could rest in the I AM consciousness, the Bodhisattva. All eight parts were to be given equal value when an aspirant undertook the path of yoga.

The eight limbs of yoga are as follows:

Yama – the practice of universal moral principles.

Niyama – the practice of personal disciplines.

Asana – the practice of physical postures.

Pranayama – the practice of breath control.

Pratyahara – the practice of withdrawal of the senses.

Dharana – the practice of focused attention.

Dhyana – the practice of meditation.

Samadhi – Enlightenment. Self-Realization.

1. The first limb, Yama is non-violence, truth, non-stealing, and taking from life what one needs, there is no room for greed here. These practices dissolve Rajas Guna and increase the level of Sattva Guna.

2. Niyama is the practice of gratitude and contentment for what we have in life, it is where we surrender the ego and learn to live as our authentic self. It is the gaining of wisdom to dissolve Tamas Guna. Sharman's say people have a lot of knowledge about the weather and rain, when it is going to rain, and how much will fall, but do they know how to make it rain?

3. Asanas are the physical postures of yoga that stretches, revitalizes, and tones the entire body, from the tips of the hands to the tips of the toes. Yoga teaches us how to listen to our body and keep it working as the body was meant to, a perfectly healthy body and mind, so we can live a life of service to others and this planet.

4. Pranayama is the cleansing and purifying of the body on a deeper level via the breath. It controls the flow of prana in the body and leads us to inner stillness by regulating the incoming and outgoing flow of breath.

5. Pratyahara is the withdrawal of the senses that enables us to switch off our senses of sight, hearing, smelling from external stimuli so that unity and stillness can flow through the whole Nervous System. 'For the mind which yields to the wandering senses carries away his wisdom as a gale carries away a ship on waters.' The Bhagavad Gita (11:66,7)

6. Dharana is total focused absorption. It is the attention with intensity that we give to our yoga practice. It requires us to let go of everything else and immerse ourselves in our yoga practice, including everything else that we do in life, so that our true capabilities can be expressed.

7. Dhyana is meditation, the stilling of the mind that allows us to experience timelessness. In dhyana, the seventh limb of the eightfold path, we experience our true self. We do not have to pretend to the outside world to be anyone else other than who we truly are. Dhyana helps us to develop a deeper insight into life as we embrace the inside and the outside world. It takes us out of linear time into sacred time, into infinity.

8. The eighth limb is Samadhi, the goal post in yoga. When we reach Samadhi, we have no thoughts or memory of harming anyone, nor are we striving to keep doing good. We have entered that state of blissfulness where all the gunas in our samskara are dissolved. The Soul has reached enlightenment. We are one with the Light that Christians call the Christ Light.

The Practice of Samanvaya Yoga is the practice of all the eight limbs of yoga, it is a sequence of yoga asanas to heal the body's central nervous system that connects to the Sushumna, the Nadis, the Guna's, and the Samskara. Throughout the yoga practice keep the focus on your breath and your yoga practice will be more successful. When we stimulate the Nervous System in a positive way via Samanvaya yoga, we re-connect with our innate goodness through a deepened awareness of our inner wisdom. The bandhas are very useful during asana practice because they work with the nervous and endocrine systems. They also prevent muscles in the buttocks and thighs from tightening (and tensing up) and causing discomfort. The Mulabundha is a muscle located at the perineum – the area between the anus and the genitals, about 2.5cm in towards the core of the body. The other bandha Uddhyanabandha is the muscle located in the core of the body just below the navel, the part above the pubic bone and below the navel. In women it is also linked to the cervix. When used regularly it can prevent prolapsed uterus from happening later in life.

This yoga practice was given to me by Yogacharya Mithai Lal Sonkar of International Yoga Training Ashram, Yognagar, Nagawa, Varanasi, India.

Samanvaya Yoga

Begin your session standing and take your focus to your feet and make sure they are firmly planted on your yoga mat. Now tighten your upper legs and buttocks and pull in the Mulabundha and keep this bandha locked in.

Place one hand on your diaphragm and the other hand on your upper chest and breathe in deeply, then exhale, now place your hands in prayer position and take a deep breath in and chant the sound Om.

Now stretch both arms up, interlocking the fingers turning the palms of your hands upwards stretching the arms from your armpits and come up on your toes and walk 3 steps forward and 3 steps back, bring your heels down and slowly bring down your arms.

Santulan – Stretch right arm up and bend the left knee and bring the left heel up to touch your bottom. Bring the leg and hand down repeat the same process with the other arm and leg.

Bend the right knee up and hold it using both hands then take the foot backwards with the knee still bent. Do the same with the other leg.

Squat against the wall with your back pressed into the wall with knees bent, like you are sitting on a chair. Fold your arms and focus on your breathing.

Stand on your mat, stretch out your arms and bring the right hand to your left foot, come up then do the other side.

Stretch & Bend, stretch the legs out as far apart as you can, bring the palms of your hands down onto the mat, and stretch and bend the legs, focusing on your breathing the whole time. Now take your legs further apart and bring your head to the mat and let it rest on your crown chakra. Place your hands behind your back, if you can.

Triangle Pose, Trikonasana – legs apart, looking up place right hand on right leg, left hand stretched up. Do other side.

Warrior Asana – Stretch legs apart, bend right knee, place right hand near foot and stretch the left arm to the front and left foot to the back. Feel the stretch in the left side of the body. Now do the other side stretching the right side.

Come to the standing pose, let your arms hang like two strings at the side of your body, allow your whole body to relax then breathe in deeply through both nostrils and let the breath out through your mouth with a sigh. Do this a few times.

Whistle breath – Breathe in deeply through both nostrils and whistle it out. 3x

Third eye breath – breathe into your third eye and breathe out 3x and let your breath get softer and softer until you can hardly feel it.

Sushumna breath, tighten your buttock muscles and breathe in through the spinal cord in your back and breathe out through the two nadis in your back, Ida and Pingala. 3x

Zen meditation walk, to heal the Vagus nerve. Hold hands behind you, lift your right leg breathing in and put it down breathing out, then do the left leg as you walk around the room for a minute.

Yogi pose. Stand on right foot with left foot on right thigh and hands in prayer position. Change sides.

Tree pose Stretch arms up with hands together and place left foot on right thigh, swap sides. From your waist drop and hang, let your body go to jelly, slowly come up and drop again.

Twist pose, Garudasana, twist right arm over left arm and right leg over left leg, then swap sides. This brings balance to the Nervous System.

Bend your body and place your fingers under your toes and lift your heels off the ground. Then come up to stand.

Surya Namaskar, stand in prayer position, stretch both arms up, then place them on your mat and take the right leg back then the left, knees, chest, chin to the mat, and go head up into the cobra pose, then bring your bottom up, like downward dog, now bring the right leg up to the front, then the left, stretch arms up and bring them back into prayer position. Repeat starting with the left leg this time.

Let your arms hang down and put your hands in to Surya Mudra (pg. 85) and focus on them slowly take your head around, then go the other way. Nod your head forward and back, and from side to side, massage the back of your neck, then drag your fingers over your neck and shoulders and flick any tension from that part of your body out of your fingers.

Upper dog, Downward dog, take both legs back with a little jump and do the cobra pose, head up, then take your bottom up, legs straight, feet on the mat and head down, gently come down onto your knees and sit down on your mat with your legs stretched out.

Focus on your ankles as you bend your feet forwards and backwards; roll your ankles, put right foot on top of left foot toes and roll right ankle, do the other foot. Now bring feet together, soles touching and do Butterfly pose by holding your feet together and flapping your knees up and down. Book pose, open feet out like a book. Look at the soles of your feet, like you are reading a book. Stretch out your legs.

Push Ups: use your arms to push your bottom up. Side push-ups-Lying on your side balance on your right arm and push your body up and stretch up your left arm then roll over and do the other side. Reclining Buddha pose: lie on your right side, legs stretched out and right arm bent with your face resting on your right hand. Lift your right leg up and down 3x. Roll over and do the left leg. Lie on your back, bend both knees and grab onto your big toes and open the legs wide; bring them together and imagine you are riding a bicycle with your legs, then back pedal. Stretch both legs up and slowly bring them down. REST, lying perfectly still for a minute or two. Roll over into Cat Pose, knees and hands on mat.

Stretch out right arm and left leg then do the other side; this balances the brain.

Sarvangabaddhasana: to balance the hormones, head on your mat, bend the knees and pull your feet up to your bottom with your hands. Come up to kneeling, right hand stretched up and left hand on left heel. Swap sides. Place hands on middle back and slightly bend backwards and forwards 3x. Camel pose: Kneeling bend backwards and place both hands on ankles. Quiet child, bring forehead on to the mat and place arms behind you. Drop the shoulders and completely relax. Bhringasana, Egyptian Spinix, bring hands and forearms on to mat, head up, and say I AM POWERFUL.

Mrigasana, deer eating grass pose, whilst kneeling lift feet and place one foot over the other, then swap feet and lift, keep your head up with arms folded behind you. With knees bent lie on your back and push your bottom up 3x. Suptavajasana-lying on your back, knees bent, stretch arms behind you, or lie on folded arms under your head. Come into the cat pose and do little bird, Bakasana, head and hands on mat, elbows high and bring your knees on to your elbows. REST.

Place a block under your back, close to your bottom, it must feel comfortable, and relax.

Janu Asana, sit on your mat stretch out your right leg and bend your left leg and place your left foot on the inner right thigh and bend your body from the waist over your stretched leg. Change legs and repeat the process. Then bend over both legs.

Bend your right knee foot on the mat, place your right hand behind you and left elbow on right knee. Turn your head over your right hand and slowly untwist your head until you are facing the front. Repeat with the left knee up and left hand behind you.

Make your hands into two tight fists and imagine you are pushing two bicycle pedals up and down. Stretch out fingers and pull and turn each finger left and right, do both hands.

Chatushkonasana, modified, carry your right leg by placing your right hand under your right knee, now with your left hand hold your right toe and with your right hand hold your left toe. Repeat changing legs.

Greeting the Earth pose, sitting up tall from your waist turn your body to the right and place your forehead, third eye, on the floor. Come back to sitting tall.

Repeat over to the left side of your body.

Sarvangasana, shoulder stand, lie on your back hugging your knees and roll from side to side then throw your legs up and take your feet over your head, backwards. Carefully bring your legs down onto the mat, knees bent.

Fish pose, bring your upper body up using your elbows, now take your head backwards and let your crown chakra touch the mat; slowly put your head flat down, and turn your head from side to side and think of your skull. Turning your head from side to side can be done often when lying on your back to remove tension from your neck. Rock up and go into the turtle pose, head tucked under near your knees. Come up to sitting and place hands under your bent knees and lift feet, lower legs up and down 3x

Boat pose, sitting up lift your feet off the mat with knees bent and stretch hands out in front of you.

Bridge pose, with feet on the mat and hands on your mat lift your bottom up to make a bridge.

Lie on your stomach with your head on your folded arms and breathe into the back of your head, the pituitary gland, and breathe out. Repeat this 3x.

Cobra pose, hands by your sides lift your body from the waist, head up then come down.

Salabasana, stretch both arms out in front of you and make both hands into tight fists, place them under your body and lift both your feet. Come out of the pose.

Makarasana, modified into the plank, hands together in one tight fist and with elbows on the mat use your toes to lift the body up and make a plank. Hold this pose for as long as you can.

Bring your body into the cat pose, on all fours, and using the breath breathe into your dropped belly then as you breathe out arch your back up as high as you can, like a cat.5x

Finish the asanas in the gratitude pose or Candle pose, by balancing your body on your toes heels up and knees bent sideways and hands in prayer position on the top of your head. Hold this pose for as long as you can and silently say thank you, thank you, thank you for the healing that has come to your body during your yoga practice, because healing happens in the body whether you are aware of it or not, or you can silently say Thank You to Adiyogi, the first yogi, for giving us the gift of yoga.

Meditation/Relaxation, this should take 5 to 10 minutes.

Lie down on your mat and let your body completely relax as you go deep within.

Chant - Shanti, Shanti, Shanti, Om

This yoga practice, if done every day will eliminate bad memories from the mind and samskara and give you a new outlook on life as your Sattva Guna energy levels increase whilst Rajas and Tamas decreases. Yoga is completely non-competitive, because it brings you into oneness with the Universe.

You have found your true Self, the Divinity within.

Index to Affirmations, Prayers, and Visualizations

Printed and bound by CPI Group (UK) Ltd, Croydon, CR0 4YY

30/04/2025

01857723-0001